SOCIAL
JUSTICE

SOCIAL JUSTICE

By

Kenneth E. Boulding

William K. Frankena

Paul A. Freund

Alan Gewirth

Gregory Vlastos

Edited by Richard B. Brandt

A SPECTRUM BOOK

Prentice-Hall, Inc.   Englewood Cliffs, N.J.

Preface

The philosophical revolution of the last decades has touched the concept of social justice only lightly. Compared with the shower of books and articles on *good* and *ought* and *right*—on what these words mean and how they can be used, and on the kind of reasoning typically marshalled in support of statements about what is moral—there have only been scattered drops on *just* and *unjust*.

The neglect of this subject does not result from a lack of importance in human thought. Nearly every day there is cause to consider whether some policy or decision is just to the stockholders, the workers, the farmers, or the consumers. Nor does it result from a dearth of outstanding problems, as if it were clear what *just* and *unjust* mean, and what are the criteria of a just action, society, economic system, set of laws, and so on. It *could* be true that the *theory* of justice is in good order, and that the only problem is strategy or tactics for realizing the ideal of justice in the social order. But in fact this is far from true. The simplest questions about *just* and *unjust* have not been answered: for instance, whether it is contradictory to say of a state of affairs that it is unjust but morally right, and whether it is contradictory to say of an action that it was unjust but violated no one's rights, or whether *just* and *fair* are synonyms (and if not, wherein their meanings differ). Much less is there agreement about what features an action or society or institution must have, in order to be called just. The one point of agreement among contemporary thinkers seems to be that equality and justice have a close relation.

The essays in this volume are a concerted effort to clear one corner of this thicket, the area of *social justice*—the problem of justice in society or of a just society. In an earlier form they were lectures delivered at Swarthmore College, under the auspices of

v

the William J. Cooper Foundation, during the spring of 1961. The authors had been invited to lecture on any aspect of the problem of social justice which seemed to them important. As it turned out, four of the lecturers chose to concern themselves with the *concept* of social justice.

This unity of topic turned out to be a happy fact. For the lecturers represent quite diverse areas of interest and experience. Three are philosophers. But of these one has had a major interest in the philosophy of politics and is known for his analysis of historic political philosophers; a second is a scholar in the field of Greek philosophy, with a second specialty in the history of social thought; and the third is primarily a moral philosopher of the contemporary analytic school. So, although all are philosophers and steeped in the tradition of Anglo-American analytic thought, they bring quite different perspectives to their task. Another of the lecturers comes from the field of law, being one of the foremost scholars on constitutional law. The fifth is a theoretical economist, whose chapters on the just distribution of economic goods have captured the attention of scholars in various fields.

The essays often do not play in harmony. This is as it should be. The book does not pretend to be the final word on this perplexing subject, whose difficulties reflect not only the complexities of English usage but the conflicting patterns of contemporary social ideals. But it does advance the theory of the subject, and the different experiences and perspectives of the authors provide a sumptuous repast for readers who would enlarge the base of their thought on social justice.

R. B. B.

CONTENTS

SOCIAL
JUSTICE

The Concept of
Social Justice

WILLIAM K. FRANKENA

*Give the king thy judgments, O God, and thy right-
eousness unto the king's son.*

Ps. 72:1

Much of history—from what Breasted has called "the dawn of
conscience" in ancient Egypt, through the Hebrew prophets, Robin
Hood, and the Levellers, to the sit-down strikes of today—may be
thought of as a "quest for social justice." The Declaration of Independence was one long appeal to "the voice of justice" against a
"train of abuses and usurpations" by the king of Great Britain. But
our present task is neither to trace the history of this quest nor to
estimate the extent to which it has been successful. It is rather to
determine the nature, the object of this quest—what is social
justice?

I. *Preliminaries*

I propose to take social justice, not as a property of individuals
and their actions, but as a predicate of societies—particularly such
societies as are called nations—and of their acts and institutions.
The terms "justice" and "injustice" may also refer to the actions of
individuals, but our concern is with their social application—with
justice and injustice writ large, to use Plato's phrase—that is, with

1

their manifestation by a society in its dealings with its individual members and subsocieties.

Although social justice will be considered as a property or virtue of national societies, it is not simply a property or virtue of such a society in its *formal*, or legal aspect—what is called the state. That is political justice, a part of social justice. But society does not consist merely of the law or the state: it has also a more *informal* aspect, comprised of its cultural institutions, conventions, moral rules, and moral sanctions. In order for a society to be fully just, it must be just in its informal as well as in its formal aspect.

Niebuhr and many other theologians usually associate justice with love. They assert, on the one hand, that justice is a function or political application of the law of love, and, on the other, that love is the fulfilment of justice. Now, it is true that in a society of love all of the demands of justice would be fulfilled. But, to use medieval terminology, they would be fulfilled *eminently*, not *formally*—that is, they would be over-fulfilled rather than literally fulfilled. Such a society would not be called unjust, of course, but it would hardly be correct to describe it as just. It seems more accurate to contrast love and justice than to link them; even the theologians referred to like to say there is a "tension" between them. I shall, therefore, here adopt the view that social justice cannot be defined in terms of love. This view is represented by Emil Brunner.[1]

> The sphere in which there are just claims, rights, debits and credits, and in which justice is therefore the supreme principle, and the sphere in which the gift of love is supreme, where there are no deserts, where love, without acknowledging any claim, gives all—these two spheres lie as far apart as heaven from hell. . . . If ever we are to get a clear conception of the nature of justice, we must also get a clear idea of it as differentiated from and contrasted with love.

That is a bit strong, as theological pronouncements sometimes are, but it is on the right track. Also it implies what is the last of my preliminary points: that social justice is not the only feature of an

<hr>

[1] *Justice and the Social Order* (London: Lutterworth Press, 1945), pp. 104, 114.

ideal society. Societies can be loving, efficient, prosperous, or good, as well as just, but they may well be just without being notably benevolent, efficient, prosperous, or good. Our problem is to define the concept of a just society, not that of an ideal society.

II. *An Ancient Formula for Justice*

To define the concept of social justice we must answer two questions which it is important to distinguish from one another. First, what are the criteria or principles of social justice? In other words, what features make or render a society just or unjust? Second, what are we doing or saying when we say of a society that it is just or unjust? Let us begin with the former. As is stated in an ancient formula, a society is just if it renders to its various members what is due them. But what is it that is due them? To reply that that is due them which is justly theirs or to which they have a right, is to add nothing. For we must still determine what it is that is their due or their right. To specify that their due or their right is what is accorded to them by the laws of the state may, speaking legally, suffice. The laws of the state, however, may be themselves unjust, and if so, it follows that social justice cannot consist wholly in their observance. Since social justice includes moral as well as legal justice, one might say that a society is just if its laws and actions conform to its moral standards. But even the prevailing moral principles of a society may be unjust or oppressive.

It may be said that a man's due or right is that which is his by virtue not merely of the law or of prevailing moral rules, but of valid moral principles, and that a society is just if it accords its members what it is required to accord them by valid moral principles. According to this view, social justice consists in the apportionment of goods and evils, rewards and punishments, jobs and privileges, in accordance with moral standards which can be shown to be valid. In other words, social justice is any system of distribution and retribution which is governed by valid moral principles. This view, if true, still leaves unsolved the very difficult question of which moral principles are valid, but at least simplifies matters by telling us that the answer to this question will provide the definition of justice. The concept of justice, it says, involves no special problems; all we have to do is to find out what is right.

This view is indeed plausible, for what could be more obvious than that a society is just if it treats its members as it ought to? And yet can justice be so simply equated with acting rightly? It does not seem to me that it can. Not all right acts—for example, acts of benevolence, mercy, or returning good for evil—can be properly described as just. Nor are all wrong acts unjust. As R. B. Brandt points out, incest may be wrong but the terms "just" and "unjust" simply do not apply.[2] Not all moral principles are "principles of justice" even if they are valid—for example, the principles J. S. Mill calls generosity and beneficence are not. Justice, then, is acting in accordance with the principles of justice; it is not simply acting in accordance with valid moral principles.

This point may be emphasized in another way. Whether justice can be defined as a process of distributing and retributing in accordance with valid moral principles seems to depend on which moral principles turn out to be valid. Suppose the so-called principle of utility is understood, as some utilitarians seem to understand it, to mean that the right course of action is simply that which produces the greatest quantitative balance of something good (say, pleasure) over something evil (say, pain) regardless of how this quantity is distributed. Suppose, furthermore, that this principle of utility turns out to be the only valid principle of morality. Then distributing and retributing in accordance with valid moral principles will not coincide with what is called justice, though it may yield what is called beneficence. Justice is not simply the greatest possible balance of pleasure over pain or of good over evil. Justice has to do, not so much with the quantity of good or evil, as with the manner in which it is distributed. Two courses of action may produce the same relative quantities of good and evil, yet one course may be just and the other unjust because of the ways in which they apportion these quantities.

Therefore, unless we depart from our ordinary understanding of

---

[2] *Ethical Theory* (Englewood Cliffs, N.J.: Prentice-Hall, Inc., 1959), p. 409. Cf. also J. Hospers, *Human Conduct* (New York: Harcourt, Brace and World, Inc., 1961), pp. 416f.

the term "justice," social justice cannot be defined merely by saying that a society is just which acts, distributes, and so on, in accordance with valid moral principles. If this is correct, however, then right-making characteristics or justifying considerations must be distinguished from just-making or justicizing considerations. Just-making considerations are only one species of right-making considerations. And, theoretically at least, a consideration of one kind may overrule a consideration of the other. In particular, a just-making consideration may be overruled by a right-making one which is not included under justice. As Portia says to Shylock,

> . . . earthly power doth then show likest God's
> When mercy seasons justice.

Furthermore, an inequality may sometimes be justified by its utility; the action or policy that promotes the inequality would then be right—but it might not be, strictly speaking, just.

It is true, as Brandt has pointed out,[3] that in such a case we should not call the action or policy unjust—that we hesitate to speak of something as unjust if we cannot also correctly speak of it as wrong. And this seems to imply that justice can be defined in terms of right-dealing after all. The answer may perhaps lie in an interesting passage in Mill. He writes that in order to save a life, "it may not only be allowable, but a duty" to do something which is contrary to the principles of justice—for example, "to steal or take by force the necessary food or medicine, or to kidnap and compel to officiate the only qualified medical practitioner." He continues:[4]

> In such cases, as we do not call anything justice which is not a virtue, we usually say, not that justice must give way to some other moral principle, but that what is just in ordinary cases is, by reason of that other principle, not just in the particular case. By this useful accommodation of language, the character of indefeasibility attributed to justice is kept

---

[3] *Op. cit.*, pp. 409f. But cf. Hospers, *op. cit.*, pp. 417, 421f.; G. Vlastos, "Justice," *Revue internationale de philosophie*, 41 (1957), p. 17.

[4] All references to Mill are to *Utilitarianism*, Ch. V. Here see, e.g., O. Piest's ed. (New York: Liberal Arts Press, 1949), pp. 68f.

up, and we are saved from the necessity of maintaining that there can be laudable injustice.

The point is that "just" and "unjust" seem to play a double role. On the one hand, they refer to certain sorts of right-making considerations as against others; on the other hand, they have much the same force as do the more general terms "right" and "wrong," so much so that one can hardly conjoin "just" and "wrong," or "right" and "unjust." It is the first of these roles which is especially important in defining the criteria of social justice, and which is neglected by the view we have been discussing.

III. *Two Other Inadequate Formulae*

A just society cannot, then, be simply identified with one which renders to its members what it is right that it render them. The concept of justice involves only a certain set of related moral principles or right-making considerations, and the present problem is to describe, if possible, their characteristic features as they apply to national societies and not merely to individuals.

But we must first consider briefly another simplistic view—that which identifies a just society with a *good-working* society whose actions, institutions, laws, and moral rules are such as to promote the greatest possible general good. This view, which seems to be maintained by some defenders of the so-called welfare state, holds that society is unjust if and only if it is not as beneficent as possible, if and only if it does not produce the maximum balance of good over evil on the whole. But is such beneficence either a necessary or a sufficient condition of justice? It is usual to distinguish—even Mill does—between the principles of justice and the principles of morality. If this distinction is made, however, and even if it is allowed—as many critics of the welfare state will not allow—that society has an obligation to be beneficent, then such beneficence, unless it falls short of a certain minimum, still is no part of social justice as such. The question is what is required of society and the state if they are to be just, not what is required if they are to be good, ideal, or to have virtues other than justice. And, to be just, they must distribute goods and evils in certain ways rather than simply maximize the quantitative balance of the one over the other. Mere beneficence, then, is neither required nor sufficient for justice, and justice cannot be identified with such beneficence.

What then are the considerations or principles which constitute justice, and what are the identifying characteristics which relate them? Mill distinguishes between the principles of justice and such other principles of morality as generosity or beneficence. But he also lists "the various modes of action and arrangements of human affairs which are classed as just or as unjust," and seeks to ascertain their distinguishing attributes:[5]

(1) It is just "to respect, unjust to violate, the *legal rights* of anyone."

(2) ". . . a second case of injustice consists in taking or withholding from any person that to which he has a *moral* right."

(3) ". . . it is . . . just that each person should obtain that (whether good or evil) which he deserves, and unjust that he should obtain a good, or be made to undergo an evil, which he does not deserve."

(4) ". . . it is . . . unjust to break faith with anyone . . . or disappoint . . . expectations raised by our own conduct. . . ."

(5) ". . . it is . . . inconsistent with justice to be partial. . . . Nearly allied to the idea of impartiality is that of *equality.* . . ."

In each case Mill allows that there are exceptions to the rule, either because some other obligation of justice overrules the one in question, or because the person concerned forfeits by his conduct the good he has been led to expect. But what have these examples of justice in common? In each instance, Mill holds, there is something which it is right to do and which some individual has a right to have done. "Justice implies something which it is not only right to do and wrong not to do, but which some individual person can claim from us as his moral right." The area of justice is that in which there are duties with correlative rights, and the considerations of justice are those which establish a duty on the one side, say society, *and* a right on the other, say an individual. For Mill this area includes gratitude, veracity, and so on, but not generosity or beneficence.

[5] *Ibid.*, pp. 47ff.

According to this common and plausible view, a society is just if and insofar as it does to its members that which it ought to do *and* that which they have a right to have done for them. But it does not wholly answer our question, for it does not tell us by what principles we may identify these rights. Mill's answer, of course, is the principle of utility, but this cannot be satisfactory according to our understanding of the principle of utility, for then he is identifying justice with beneficence after all. Indeed, it seems satisfactory to Mill himself only because he understands the principle of utility as having the maxims of impartiality and equality built into it.[6]

IV. *Acceptable but Formal Criteria of Justice*

Mill's mention of impartiality and equality, and the traditional depiction of justice as blindfolded, suggest another conception of social justice: namely, that it is the treatment of similar cases in a similar fashion, while injustice is the treatment of similar cases in different ways. Sidgwick and Perelman especially emphasize this formula,[7] and a paradigm situation involved in questions of justice does seem to be one in which two similar cases are treated alike or differently. Different treatment is unjust unless the cases are different. That similar cases should be handled similarly does, then, seem to be part of the essence of justice. Perelman contends—rightly, I think—that this rule of justice is simply a requirement of reason, which in science and in conduct alike demands that the same be said or done with respect to instances of the same kind.[8] But, as Perelman also points out, this formula is purely formal. It says only that a society to be just must have rules and act on them. It does not say what the rules should be, or how cases of any given sort should be dealt with. All sorts of injustices may be enshrined in the rules of society, as those who settled this country knew and as

[6] For a good statement of Mill's confusion see Hospers, *op. cit.*, p. 425. Cf. Mill, *op. cit.*, pp. 66ff.

[7] H. Sidgwick, *The Methods of Ethics*, 7th ed. (London: The Macmillan Company Ltd.: 1907), pp. 379f., 386f. Cf. Perelman, *De la Justice* (Brussels: Université Libre de Bruxelles, 1945), pp. 27, 53.

[8] "La Règle de Justice," *Dialectica*, 14 (1960), p. 231; "*L'Idée de Justice*," *Annales de l'Institut Internationale de Philosophie Politique* (1959), III, p. 128.

The Concept of Social Justice　　　　　　　　　　9

many of those whose ancestors did not come willingly know even now. Even if, in the spirit of what is called "equity," society permits exceptions to its rules, allows for extenuating circumstances, and listens to excuses—as any just society must—it may still be an unjust society. In Perelman's terms, it may be formally just, but materially unjust.

Much of this applies to what C. I. Lewis calls "the fundamental dictum of justice" or "the Law of Moral Equality," which holds that "no rule of action is right except one which is right in all instances, and therefore right for everyone." [9] It insists, correctly, that the rules of a just society must be universalizable, but this is only a formal requirement. As Lewis himself points out, his dictum does not delineate the content of social justice; for that, more substantive ethical principles are required, plus "additional premises concerning human nature and human good."

V. *Equality and Justice*

Justice, whether social or not, seems to have at its center the notion of an allotment of something to persons—duties, goods, offices, opportunities, penalties, punishments, privileges, roles, status, and so on. Moreover, at least in the case of distributive justice, it seems centrally to involve the notion of *comparative* allotment. In the paradigm case, two things, A and B, are being allotted to two individuals, C and D, A to C and B to D. Whether justice is done depends on how A's being given to C compares with B's being given to D. In this sense Aristotle was right in saying that justice involves a proportion in which A is to B as C is to D. It is a requirement both of reason and of common thinking about justice that similar cases be treated similarly. This means that if C and D are similar, then A and B must be similar. But, if this is so, then it would appear that justice also demands that if C and D are dissimilar, then A and B must be dissimilar. That is to say, justice is comparative.

Actually, of course, justice does not require that all similarities and dissimilarities be respected in this way. We do not regard it as

[9] *An Analysis of Knowledge and Valuation* (La Salle, Ill.: Open Court Publishing Co., 1946), p. 482. Cf. also *The Ground and Nature of the Right* (New York: Columbia University Press, 1955), pp. 90-96.

unjust to treat similar blocks of wood dissimilarly or dissimilar ones similarly: we are concerned only about human beings (and possibly animals). Even in the case of human beings, however, justice does not call for similar treatment of every similarity or for dissimilar treatment of every dissimilarity. We do not think it is necessarily unjust, even if other things are equal, to deal similarly with people of different colors or dissimilarly with people of the same color. In fact, the historical quest for social justice has consisted largely of attempts to eliminate certain dissimilarities as bases for difference of treatment and certain similarities as bases for sameness of treatment. That is, it seems to be part of the concept of justice that not all similarities justify (or justicize) similar treatment or all differences different treatment. The point of the quest for social justice has not been merely that similarities and differences in people have too often been arbitrarily ignored; it has been mainly that the wrong similarities and differences have been taken as a basis for action. Similarities and differences should form the basis of action if it is to be just, but not all of them are relevant. The question is "Which of them are just- or unjust-making? Which of them are relevant? And is there a relation between them?"

It is important to remember that not all morally justifying considerations are just-making or justicizing. "Relevant" considerations in matters of justice cannot therefore be identified with "moral" ones, as D. D. Raphael does.[10] And it will not do to say, as Brandt does, that justice consists in treating people equally except as unequal treatment is justified by *moral* considerations of substantial weight in the circumstances.[11] If I am right, this description should be revised: justice is treating persons equally, except as unequal treatment is required by *just-making* considerations (i.e., by principles of *justice,* not merely *moral* principles) of substantial weight in the circumstances. With this emendation, the description seems to me to be correct, both in theory and as a reflection of the ordinary notion of justice. The only question then is whether there are any principles of *justice* which overrule the principle of equality,

[10] "Equality and Equity," *Philosophy,* XXI (1946), p. 5.
[11] *Op. cit.,* p. 410.

what they are, and whether they are such as to render the principle of equality otiose or not.

So far treating people equally has been equated with treating them similarly or in the same way. But suppose that society is allotting musical instruments to *C* and *D,* and that *C* prefers a banjo and *D* a guitar. If society gives *C* a banjo and *D* a guitar it is treating them *differently* yet *equally.* If justice is equal treatment of all men, then it is treatment which is equal in this sense and not simply identical. Surely neither morality nor justice, however stuffy and universalizing they may be in the eyes of Nietzsche and the existentialists, can require such monotony as identical treatment would involve. It is hard to believe that even the most egalitarian theory of justice calls for complete uniformity and not merely for substantial equality. I shall, therefore, speak in terms of equality, except when it does not matter or when it is necessary to speak in terms of similarity of treatment.

What considerations, and especially what similarities and dissimilarities in people, are just- (or unjust-) making? It is agreed that justice prescribes equals to equals and unequals to unequals, but what are the relevant respects in which people must be equal or unequal for treatment of them to be just or unjust? I have anticipated an at least partially egalitarian answer to this question, but the classical reply of Plato, Aristotle, and their many followers was different. According to them, social justice does not involve any kind of equal allotment to all men. Justice is not linked with any quality in which men are all necessarily similar or which they all share by virtue of being men. It is tied to some property which men may or may not have, and which, in fact, they have in varying amounts or degrees or not at all. Justice simply is the apportionment of what is to be apportioned in accordance with the amount or degree in which the recipients possess some required feature—personal ability, desert, merit, rank, or wealth.

This position has lately been maintained by Sir David Ross and, inconsistently, I think, by Brunner.[12] According to W. B. Gallie, it is

---

[12] W. D. Ross, *The Right and the Good* (Oxford: The Clarendon Press, 1930), pp. 26f.; Brunner, *op. cit.,* pp. 29ff.

characteristic of "liberal" as against "socialist" morality.[13] It is, however, not necessarily inegalitarian in substance; how inegalitarian it turns out to be depends on how unequal it finds men to be in the respect which it takes as basic. If it found them to be equal in this respect it would in practice have to be egalitarian, but, of course, it would not be taking equality of treatment for all men, or indeed any pair of men, as a basic requirement of justice. In this respect it may represent the classical concept of social justice, but, as Gallie and Vlastos have pointed out,[14] it hardly does justice to the modern concept in which, as Mill's list shows, equality of treatment (not merely the equal treatment of equals, but the equal treatment of all human beings as such) is one of the basic principles of justice. It is, however, true, as Gallie, Vlastos, and Mill recognize, that the modern concept of social justice is complex and includes a meritarian as well as an egalitarian element. It recognizes the demand to respect differences between persons as well as the demand to respect personality as such.[15]

Views which accept the principle of equality as a basic and at least *prima facie* requirement of justice may, of course, take less complex forms. It might be held, for example, that justice calls for a strict equality in the treatment of C and D, no matter who C and D are, and that no inequality is ever justified. Or it might be maintained that, although inequalities are sometimes justified and right, they are never just. Every departure from complete equality would then be regarded as beyond the pale of justice, though not beyond that of the morally right or obligatory. Such theories are possible and have an apparent simplicity, but they limit the usual scope of justice. Not every departure from equality is ordinarily regarded as a departure from justice, let alone from morality. For one thing, such departures are allowed on the ground of differences in ability,

---

[13] "Liberal Morality and Socialist Morality," *Philosophy, Politics and Society,* ed. Peter Laslett (Oxford: Basil Blackwell, 1956), p. 123.

[14] Gallie, *op. cit.,* pp. 122, 129; Vlastos, *op. cit.,* p. 9.

[15] This complexity may, perhaps, have the following justification. The formal rule of reason which we took to be central to justice, insofar as it is comparative, has two parts: to treat similars similarly and to treat dissimilars dissimilarly. The egalitarian principle may be regarded as a way of specifying the first part, and the meritarian as a way of specifying the second.

merit, or desert. Certain other departures from a direct or simple equality, called for by differences in need, or involved in carrying out agreements, covenants, contracts, and promises, are also recognized as just, and not merely as justified or right.

Much more reasonable, as well as closer to ordinary thinking, is the conception of social justice as the equal treatment of all persons, except as inequality is required by relevant—that is, just-making—considerations or principles. This is the view which I accepted as an emendation of Brandt's. It takes equality of treatment to be a basic *prima facie* requirement of justice, but allows that it may on occasion be overruled by other principles of justice (or by some other kind of moral principle). This view, however, is not necessarily very egalitarian. It does hold that all men are to be treated equally and that inequalities must be justified. But it also allows that inequalities may be justified, and everything depends on the ease and the kinds of considerations by which they may be justified. In fact, it tells us very little until it gives us answers to the following questions: What is meant by equal or similar treatment? What considerations are relevant to the justification of inequalities or dissimilarities? Are there any respects in which men are actually to be treated equally or similarly, or is this requirement always overruled by other considerations? Are there not always differences in personality, need, desert, merit, which completely nullify the *prima facie* rule of equality?

VI. *Other Principles of Justice and Their Relation to Equality*

The concept of social justice which prevails in our culture has now been partly defined. According to this concept, a society is without justice insofar as it is without rules (statutes or precedents, written or unwritten rules, legal and moral rules); it must, in both its formal and informal aspects, treat similar cases similarly. It must also treat human beings equally, or it must show why—a requirement which governs its rules as well as its acts and institutions. That is, the primary similarity to be respected is that which all men, as such, have. But a just society must also respect some though not all differences. In particular it must respect differences in capacities and needs, and in contribution, desert, or merit. Such differences may often make it just to treat people unequally in certain respects, thus at least qualifying the *prima facie* requirement of equality. But many other differences—for example, differences in blood or color— are not just-making. The recognition of capacity and need and the recognition of contribution and desert are not, however, the only principles of justice which may qualify the principle of equality. There is also the principle that agreements should be kept.

Are there any other principles of social justice besides the principle of equality, that of recognizing capacity and need, and that of keeping agreements? I have argued that the principle of beneficence or utility is not a principle of justice, though it is a moral principle. That is, a society is not unjust if it is not by its own direct action bringing about the greatest possible balance of good over evil. It is still, however, an old and familiar view (which I accept) that it is unjust for society or the state to injure a citizen, to withhold a good from him, or to interfere with his liberty (except to prevent him from committing a crime, to punish him for committing one, or to procure the money and other means of carrying out its just functions), and that this is unjust even if society or the state deals similarly with all of its citizens. It seems to me also that a society is unjust if, by its actions, laws, and mores, it unnecessarily impoverishes the lives of its members materially, aesthetically, or otherwise, by holding them to a level below that which some members at least might well attain by their own efforts. If such views are correct, we must add to the principles of social justice those of noninjury, non-interference, and non-impoverishment.

These additions make it harder to discover what it is, if anything, that relates these principles of justice. It has sometimes been argued, however, that they are linked in that they all involve and ultimately depend on a recognition of the equality or equal intrinsic value of every human personality—or at least that they do so insofar as they are principles of justice. If this could be established, the area of justice could then be described as the area of moral reasoning in which the final appeal is to the ideal of the equality of all men.

There is much to be said for this suggestion. Raphael, for instance, has very plausibly contended that differences in treatment on grounds of special need may be construed as attempts to restore inequalities due to natural or extraneous causes.[16] This would account for the justice of giving special attention to people—for example, those who are disabled or mentally backward—who are, for no fault of their own, at a disadvantage with respect to others.

More generally, it seems as if much, if not all, of the justice of recognizing differences in capacity, need, and so on, might be accounted for in terms of the ideal of equality, as follows. One of the chief considerations which not only justifies but also establishes as *just* differences in the treatment of human beings is the fact that the good life (not in the sense of the morally good life but in the sense, roughly, of the happy life) and its conditions are not the same for all, due to their differences in needs and potentialities. I am inclined to think that it is this fact, rather than that of differences in ability, merit, and the like, which primarily justifies differences in the handling of individuals. It is what justifies, for example, giving *C* a banjo, *D* a guitar, and *E* a skin-diving outfit. Although *C, D,* and *E* are treated differently, they are not dealt with unequally, since their differing needs and capacities so far as these relate to the good life are equally considered and equally well cared for. The ideal of equality itself may require certain differences of treatment, including, for example, differences in education and training. The principle involved in this claim is independent of the principle of recognizing differences in merit, but also of the principle of utility. For the differences in treatment involved are not justified simply by arguing that they are conducive to the general good life (though they may also be justified in this way), but by arguing that they are required for the good lives of the individuals concerned. It is not as if one must first look to see how the general good is best subserved and only then can tell what treatment of individuals is just. Justice entails the presence of equal *prima facie* rights prior to any consideration of *general* utility.

Yet inequalities and differences in treatment are often said to be justified by their general utility. I do not deny this, but I do doubt

[16] *Op. cit.,* p. 9.

that they can be shown to be *just* merely by an appeal to general utility. They can, however, often be shown to be just by an argument which is easily confused with that from the principle of utility: that initial inequalities in the distribution of offices, rewards, and so on, are required for the promotion of equality in the long run. In fact, much of what still needs to be done consists not so much of building up the biggest possible balance of welfare over illfare as in promoting the conditions for its equal distribution. It therefore seems plausible that much, if not all, of the justification of differences of function, as well as of the recognition of ability, contribution, merit, and need—at least insofar as these may be denominated "just"—is based on such an indirect appeal to the ideal of equality. It also seems plausible that the introduction of incentives into economic and social systems, the redistribution of wealth through progressive taxation, and the reformation of the law may be *justicized,* if at all, only by such a line of argument, even if they may also be *justified* on other grounds.

If the duty to keep faith is assumed to be a requirement of justice, can it be justified in terms of the principle of equality? It does seem as if the practice of keeping promises and fulfilling contracts may be at least partly justified—and justicized—by such an indirect appeal to the promotion of equality. But perhaps the breaking of a promise can also be called unjust on the ground that it entails a direct violation of equality. The man who makes a promise and then breaks it, presumably for his own interest, is not only violating a useful practice but also favoring his good life over that of the others involved in the practice—in short, he is not treating persons as equals.

Retributive justice—for example, punishment—must also be considered. Aristotle and others have brought it under the principle of equality by contending that the retribution restores the equality between the offender and the injured which had been disturbed. It might also be contended that, having violated the principle of equality, the criminal may justly be regarded as having forfeited his claim to a good life on equal terms with others, and even his claim not to be pained. Critics of the retributive theory of punishment might prefer to argue that punishment is made just, and perhaps also obligatory, by the fact that it tends to promote the most equality in the long run by preventing people from infringing on the claims of others. This is a non-utilitarian line of reasoning which looks not to the past, but to the future—not to future welfare, but to future equality.

There is, then, a good deal to be said for the suggestion that the principles of justice are distinguished from other principles of morality by being governed by the ideal of equality. Certainly the *prima facie* duty of treating people as equals is not rendered otiose because it so often permits inequalities of one sort or another. Nevertheless, G. F. Hourani may not be wholly right when he says that justice is equality "evident or disguised." [17] The claims of special desert may remain at least partially recalcitrant to such an interpretation. But even if Raphael's conclusion that the unequal treatment called for by special desert is a "real deviation from equality," [18] is false, there still remain the principles of non-injury, non-interference, and non-impoverishment. Although the rule that a just society must provide a certain minimum level of welfare for everyone may be construed as an offshoot of the rule of equality, violations of these negative principles are unjust but do not necessarily entail any inequality of treatment, direct or indirect. If a ruler were to boil his subjects in oil, jumping in afterward himself, it would be an injustice, but there would be no inequality of treatment.

It might be argued that the injustice involved depends on an inequality after all because the ruler did not permit his subjects to participate in the decision to commit national suicide. And perhaps it might be further argued that whenever society or the state injures, interferes, or impoverishes unjustly, the injustice consists in the fact that it does not provide the individuals victimized an equal share in the process of decision-making. Then, excepting possibly the principle of recognizing desert, the principles of justice might all be claimed to rest, directly or indirectly, on the ideal of equality. I should myself welcome this conclusion, but it seems that a so-called primitive society might be so bound by tradition that although all its members had a substantially equal voice in all decisions its rules

[17] *Ethical Value* (Ann Arbor: University of Michigan Press, 1955), p. 86.
[18] *Op. cit.*, p. 10.

might nevertheless be unnecessarily restrictive or injurious, and therefore unjust.

If not all of these principles can be subsumed under equality, it might be argued that the recalcitrant ones should not be regarded as principles of justice, however valid they may be as moral principles. This strikes me as a rather drastic bit of conceptual legislation. Though such a departure from our ordinary understanding of social justice may be desirable in the interests of neatness, and not objectionable in principle, I am inclined to think that there is a less radical alternative.

VII. *Basic Theory of Justice*

What we need at this point is a plausible line of thought that will explain both the role of equality in the concept of justice and those principles of justice which are not derivable from the ideal of equality. With the rule of non-interference with liberty particularly in mind, H. L. A. Hart has maintained that the sphere of justice and rights coincides not with that of equality, but with that in which the final appeal is to the claim to equal liberty for all.[19] Using a more positive conception of liberty, Raphael contends similarly that the essential points of justice and liberty are the same. The claims of desert and equality are both subsumed under the one concept of justice, he thinks, because both are concerned with protecting the interests of the individual, and so their concern is basically that of liberty.[20] Following a somewhat different line of thought, S. M. Brown argues that justice requires of society only that it provide institutions protecting the moral interests, persons, and estates of its members.[21] By restating what I take to be a familiar position, I shall not so much question as supplement these conclusions. In doing so I propose to argue that the principles of the family of justice, insofar as they go beyond the requirements of equality, direct or indirect, go beyond them only because they ex-

---

[19] "Are There Any Natural Rights?" *Philosophical Review*, LXIV (1955), pp. 177ff.

[20] *Moral Judgment* (London: Allen & Unwin Ltd., 1955), pp. 67, 94.

[21] "Inalienable Rights," *Philosophical Review*, LXIV (1955), pp. 192-211.

press a certain limited concern for the good lives of individual persons as such.

In opposition to the classical meritarian view of social justice, I accepted as part of my own view the principle that all men are to be treated as equals, not because they are equal in any respect but simply because they are human. They are human because they have emotions and desires, and are able to think, and hence are capable of enjoying a good life in a sense in which other animals are not. They are human because their lives may be "significant" in the manner which William James made so graphic in his essays "On a Certain Blindness in Human Beings" and "What Makes a Life Significant?":

> Wherever a process of life communicates an eagerness to him who lives it, there the life becomes genuinely significant. Sometimes the eagerness is more knit up with the motor activities, sometimes with the perceptions, sometimes with the imagination, sometimes with reflective thought. But, wherever it is found . . . there *is* importance in the only real and positive sense in which importance ever anywhere can be.[22]

By the good life is meant not so much the morally good life as the happy or satisfactory life. As I see it, it is the fact that all men are similarly capable of enjoying a good life in this sense that justifies the *prima facie* requirement that they be treated as equals. To quote James again, "The practical consequence of such a philosophy [as is expressed in the passage just cited] is the well-known democratic respect for the sacredness of individuality. . . ."[23] It seems plausible to claim, however, that this insight (which Royce calls "moral" and James "religious") into the "sacredness" of human beings justifies not only their equal treatment but also a real, even if limited, concern for the goodness of their lives. It justifies treating them not only as equals but also, at least in certain ways, as ends.

A just society, then, is one which respects the good lives of its members and respects them equally. A just society must therefore promote equality; it may ignore certain differences and similarities but must consider others; and it must avoid unnecessary injury,

[22] *Talks to Teachers on Psychology, and to Students on Some of Life's Ideals* (New York: Holt, Rinehart, and Winston, Inc., 1899), pp. 264f.

[23] *Ibid.*, pp. vf.

interference, or impoverishment—all without reference to beneficence or general utility. The demand for equality is built into
the very concept of justice. The just society, then, must consider
and protect the good life of each man equally with that of any
other, no matter how different these men may be, and so it must
allow them equal consideration, equal opportunity, and equality
before the law. The equal concern for the good lives of its members
also requires society to treat them differently, for no matter
how much one believes in a common human nature, individual
needs and capacities differ, and what constitutes the good life for
one individual may not do so for another. It is the society's very
concern for the good lives of its members that determines which
differences and which similarities it must respect (and which are
relevant to justice). A society need not respect those differences
which have only an *ad hoc* bearing or none at all, on the good lives
of their possessors—for example, color of skin. But it must respect
differences like preferring one religion to another, which do have a
bearing on the individual good life.

None of this implies that society may impose or presuppose any
fixed conception of the good life. As James says, "The pretension
to dogmatize about [this] is the root of most human injustices and
cruelties. . . ." [24] Nor does it mean that society must seek to make
the life of one man as good as that of any other, for men may well
be so different that the best life of which one is capable is not as
good as that of which another is capable. The good lives open to
men may not be equally good—even if they are called incommen-
surable they may still not be equally good. Nevertheless, they must
be equally respected and protected. That is why I reject Rashdall's
formula for justice, that "every man's good [is] to count as equal to
the *like good* of every other man," [25] for this suggests that two people
are to be treated as equals only if they are capable of equally good
lives. It is more accurate, in my opinion, to say that the just society
must insofar as possible make *the same relative contribution* to the
good life of every individual—except, of course, in cases of reward
and punishment, and provided that a certain minimum standard

[24] *Ibid.,* p. 265.
[25] H. Rashdall, *The Theory of Good and Evil* (London: Oxford University
Press, 1907), I, p. 240.

has been achieved by all. This is what I understand as the recognition of equal intrinsic value of individual human beings.

But the regard which the just society must have for the good lives of its members involves more than equal treatment. If I am right, it does not involve direct action on the part of society to promote the good life of its members, whether this be conceived of as pleasure, happiness, self-realization, or some indefinable quality. Such direct action is beneficence, not justice. Nevertheless, a just society must be concerned for the goodness of its members' lives, and not merely for their equality, though in a more limited way than beneficence implies. A just society must protect each member from being injured or interfered with by others, and it must not, by omission or commission, itself inflict evil upon any of them, deprive them of goods which they might otherwise gain by their own efforts, or restrict their liberty—except so far as is necessary for their protection or the achievement of equality. Although we are speaking of the *just* society, and not of the *good* society, its concern with the goodness of the lives of its members need not be considered merely negative and protective. It seems reasonable to assign to the just society a more positive interest (though one which falls short of beneficence) by saying that it must, so far as possible, provide equally the conditions under which its members can by their own efforts (alone or in voluntary associations) achieve the best lives of which they are capable. This means that the society must at least maintain some minimum standard of living, education, and security for all its members.

Social justice then does not, as Ross thinks, consist *simply* in the apportionment of happiness or good life in accordance with the recipient's degree of moral goodness. In fact, society must for the most part allow virtue to be its own reward, else it is not virtue.[26] In the poem, "Easter," Arthur Clough complains that the world

> . . . visits still
> With equalest apportionment of ill
> Both good and bad alike, and brings to one same dust
> The just and the unjust.

[26] Cf. Rashdall, *op. cit.*, pp. 256ff.

Society, however, must be wary of taking on the whole enterprise of cosmic or poetic justice.[27] It must honor first of all the so-called intrinsic dignity of man, which is not the same as his moral worth. Still, it is difficult to deny that the recognition of differences in desert, merit, and service, in the form of reward and punishment and unequal apportionment, is one of the principles of social justice. It remains, therefore, to see how this principle—insofar as it is a requirement of justice and not merely of utility—can be provided for by our basic theory. It has already been suggested that recognition of this principle is required for the promotion of equality in the long run. It seems to be required also for protection, one of the duties of a just society. Punishments have often been plausibly justicized on this ground, but so may rewards and privileges of various kinds. The good life of one member of society is not independent of what other members do or do not do. Certain forms of reward may in themselves show respect for individual freedom and goodness of life, by protecting one member against the acts or failures to act on the part of others, or by guaranteeing that individual talents shall not be lost or squandered.

More might be said on this point, but it is clear that a recognition of desert, contribution, or merit can be justicized without appealing either to an ultimate principle of retribution or to the principle of beneficence. This theory of social justice lies between those of the classical liberals and those of the more extreme welfare theorists. The one group includes too little under justice, the other too much. Both tend to equate just-making or justicizing considerations with right-making or justifying ones, but classical liberals greatly restrict the range of *justified* social action while the welfare theorists unduly extend that of *justicized* social action. I hold that justice includes a more positive concern for equality and goodness of life than the classical liberals allow, and that the area of right social action may extend even further in a welfare direction. I am not so much concerned to deny the conclusions the welfare theorists draw about what society and the state may or should do—I mean to leave this an open question—as to argue that they cannot plausibly defend them all as requirements of justice.

[27] Cf. Hospers, *op. cit.*, pp. 462ff.

A just society is, strictly speaking, not simply a loving one. It must in its actions and institutions fulfil certain formal requirements dictated by reason rather than love; it must be rule-governed in the sense that similars are treated similarly and dissimilars dissimilarly. But only certain similarities and differences are relevant: those relating to the good life, merit, and so on. To a considerable extent, the recognition of these differences and similarities is required by the very ideal of equality, which is part of the concept of justice. But there are other principles of justice as well. Social justice is the equal (though not always similar) treatment of all persons, at least in the long run. This equal treatment must be qualified in the light of certain principles: the recognition of contribution and desert, the keeping of agreements, non-injury, non-interference, non-impoverishment, protection, and perhaps the provision and improvement of opportunity. These principles seem to go beyond the requirements of equality, even in the long run—but, insofar as they are principles of justice, they may be roughly unified under a conception of social justice as involving a somewhat vaguely defined but still limited concern for the goodness of people's lives, as well as for their equality. This double concern is often referred to as respect for the intrinsic dignity or value of the human individual. This is not the position of the extreme egalitarian but it is essentially egalitarian in spirit; in any case it is not the position of the meritarian, although it does seek to accommodate his principles.

Is this account of social justice normative, an ethical commitment or proposal on my part, or is it descriptive, an attempt merely to delineate the ordinary concept of social justice? It is both. It incorporates my own normative judgment, but it seeks to defend this judgment as far as possible as one which is already embodied in the ordinary view of the problem. The validity of this defense and the nature of any further defense that may be called for will be at least partly exhibited in the following concluding section.

VIII. *The Semantics of Justice*

We have sought to define the criteria or principles of social justice and the characteristics which unite them. A second, more semantical, problem is to discover what is being done or said when a society or social institution is called just or unjust. Other related questions arise: what is the ground or justification for the principle of equality and the other principles of justice? What is the validity of our conception of justice? These questions raise a problem which is not peculiar to the principles of justice; it concerns the justification and validity of basic ethical principles in general. I cannot try to solve it now, but I shall say something about it.

The concept of social justice has been defined in the sense of defining the related criteria which govern or should govern the judgment of a society or social institution as just or unjust. Now the meaning and not merely the criteria of justice must be defined. The first problem may be posed as follows: the fact that *A* has promised to do *X* is usually regarded as making it *right* that he do *X*. Two things may therefore be said of *X*: that it keeps a promise, and that it is right. Now, if *X* is said to be *just,* is this like saying that *X* fulfills a promise or like saying that *X* is right? Raphael seems to take the former interpretation; that is, he seems to regard justice as a right-making property like telling the truth or keeping a promise.[28] If this is correct, the meaning and the criteria of justice coincide, for to say that *X* is just is simply to say that *X* assigns things in accordance with merit, desert, or whatever is taken as the criterion of justice.

I prefer Brandt's interpretation, which takes the position that saying "X is just" is like saying "X is right," rather than like saying "X was promised." [29] One might use here something like G. E. Moore's open question or naturalistic fallacy arguments, but these have never seemed to me to be very decisive. It does seem to me, however, that "just" and "unjust" are more like "good," "beautiful," and their opposites, than like "tells the truth" or "keeps promises." As Brandt puts it,[30] to say that *X* is just or unjust is not simply to say that it is a certain kind of act or that it has a certain kind of effect, it is saying something "vaguer or more abstract"—the sort of thing that ethical words like "right" and "wrong" are used to say.

[28] Cf. *op. cit.,* pp. 462ff.   [29] *Op. cit.,* p. 409.
[30] *Loc. cit.*

At the same time I hold that, except for the complication noted earlier, "X is just" has a narrower and less vague meaning than "X is right." I suggest, then, that "X is just" is not equivalent to "X is equal treatment" nor to "X is right," but is like saying "X is right by virtue of being equal treatment, and so on," or, perhaps better, like saying "X is right" with the contextual implication that it is equal treatment, and so on. It has often been held by moral philosophers of late that to say "X is right" is in some sense to imply that there are good reasons for doing X. In a similar way, I think, saying that X is just implies that there are good reasons for doing it, but it implies that these reasons all belong to the set of criteria which we have been trying to specify. Saying that X is just is not simply saying that X has certain properties which are in fact just-making, but rather that X is right *qua* having those properties.

If this is true, however, then "just" has much of the force of "right." It has at least the force of "prima facie right," and since the principles of justice are especially stringent, it often has some of the force of "actually right"—so much so that we hesitate to say an act is unjust if it violates a principle of justice but is made right by other moral considerations. What is the force of the term "right" or of sentences in which it is used? There has been a great controversy about this among twentieth century philosophers—between intuitionists like G. E. Moore, naturalists like R. B. Perry, emotivists like A. J. Ayer and C. L. Stevenson, and others like S. E. Toulmin, R. M. Hare, and P. H. Nowell-Smith, not to mention John Dewey. I cannot possibly resolve this controversy here. I do not think that moral judgments of the form "X is right" are purely cognitive in content or function; they involve something like prescribing or recommending. But neither do I think that they are mere expressions or evocations of emotion, attitude, or desire, or that they are mere commands. As H. D. Aiken, A. C. Ewing, Toulmin, and others have emphasized, moral judgments claim a certain authority and support; they claim to be backed by reasons which are generally valid, or at least to have certain consensus in their favor. Hume says:

> . . . when [one] bestows on any man the epithets of *vicious* or *odious* or *depraved*, he then speaks another language [than that of self-love],

and expresses sentiments in which he expects all his audience are to concur with him. He must here . . . depart from his private and particular situation, and must choose a point of view, common to him and others.[31]

Hume goes on to suggest that our language has had to invent "a peculiar set of terms" to use when we depart from our private and particular situations and choose a point of view common to ourselves and others. He is referring only to moral terms, but a similar claim could be made for terms like "true" and "beautiful." All such terms are used to appeal beyond individual feelings and beliefs to the intersubjective consensus of rational beings or, perhaps, to the judgment of an impartial spectator. To use any of these evaluative terms is *ipso facto* to recognize some kind of supra-individual court of appeal.

If this general approach is correct, then "just" and "unjust" are among the terms used to put reactions to public test, claiming that they will pass a certain kind of test but implying that they will be revised if they do not. A. K. Rogers is probably right when he asserts that "justice" is, in one aspect, a tool for securing what is desired, "a fighting concept, incidental to the process of reform, and necessary, with a continual change of content in detail, so long as men are engaged in experimenting to find out the conditions under which they can enjoy the fullest and freest life." But, as he also says, it is a "social concept," a "concept of reason" which involves entering the lists of rational discussion and being ready to generalize any claims made or any reasons given. It is "a militant concept, not primarily a theoretical one," which calls for a peaceful campaign of rational consideration and carries the "weight of legitimacy" which only a victor in such a campaign can claim.[32] More specifically, as I see it, when we say that something in society is just or unjust, we are purporting to judge it from a point of view which is fully free, informed, and rational, transcends both ourselves and our actual society, and is committed to a respect for the good life of

[31] David Hume, *An Enquiry Concerning the Principles of Morals,* Section IX, Part I.
[32] Cf. Rogers, *The Theory of Ethics* (New York: The Macmillan Company, 1922), pp. 195, 192, 181.

every individual. And we are in some sense implying that every one else who so judges will eventually agree with us.

Some writers have maintained that the most basic principles of justice (or at least those that are substantive and not merely formal) cannot be justified and either have only a relative validity or rest on an ultimately arbitrary act of faith. Thus Perelman writes:

> . . . if justice appears as the sole rational virtue, opposing itself to the irregularity of our acts and to the arbitrariness of our rules, it must not be forgotten that its claim is itself based on values which are arbitrary and irrational, and which are opposed by other values. . . .[33]

Similarly, Isaiah Berlin says, at the end of a symposium on equality, "Like all human ends it cannot itself be defended or justified, for it is itself that which justifies other acts. . . ."[34] And Benn and Peters, discussing the question of whether the principle of equal consideration extends to all men or only to a certain class or race of men, remark that:

> When discussion reveals disagreements at the very root of morality, rational moral argument must give way to the persuasive methods of preacher and prophet. At this level, to adopt a moral position is to make an ultimate choice—i.e., one in its nature beyond the limits of rational justification, where appeals must necessarily be to the sympathetic emotions.[35]

It does not seem to me that this conclusion can be escaped by appealing to metaphysics or theology—for example, by offering, as Brunner does, the doctrine that all men are children of God or loved by God as a proof that all men are to be accounted equal. For the premise does not logically entail the desired conclusion and is itself an act of faith of just the kind that the one appealing to it is trying to avoid in the conclusion.

Nevertheless, I find it hard to accept the view that the principles of justice are arbitrary and irrational. It says, in effect, that the

---

[33] *De la Justice*, p. 81.
[34] "Equality," *Proceedings of the Aristotelian Society* (1956), p. 326.
[35] S. I. Benn and R. S. Peters, *Social Principles and the Democratic State* (London: Allen and Unwin, Ltd., 1959), p. 116.

most basic convictions expressible in ethical terms are not subject
to the very kind of public debate for which these terms were in-
vented. To say this, however, is to assume that the claim which is
made by the use of ethical terms is false, namely, the claim that all
those who are free, fully informed, and rational, and who take a
point of view common to themselves and others, will eventually
agree. Yet this claim has never actually been shown to be false, and
it seems to me that, until it is, we may and, in fact, should continue
to cherish the hope for a rational consensus of which Hume spoke
so wisely.[36]

Even the most basic principles of justice then, claim (and, one
may hope, not in vain) that they will be sustained by all who make
a full and free review of them from the common point of view
which is presupposed by all our moral judgments.[37] If anything like
this is true, then such principles can be thought of as having a
genuine validity which transcends the individuals who express them
and makes it possible for these individuals to criticize their social
institutions. Brunner contends that all judgment of social institutions as just or unjust presupposes an unwritten, eternal, divine
law or standard which transcends all human legislation and is binding on all societies:

> Whoever says with serious intent, "That is just" or "That is unjust"
> has . . . appealed to a standard which transcends all human laws, con-
> tracts, customs and usages, a standard by which all these human stand-
> ards are measured. Either this absolute, divine justice exists or else
> justice is merely another word for something which suits some but not
> others. . . . Either the word *justice* refers to the primal ordinance of
> God, and has the ring of holiness and absolute validity, or it is a tink-
> ling cymbal and sounding brass.[38]

Here Brunner makes a profound point, though he overstates it.
Judgments of social justice do presuppose principles which in some

[36] Perelman himself expresses this faith or hope at the end of the first article
referred to in footnote no. 8.
[37] John Rawls implies something of this sort in a penetrating paper which
otherwise moves on somewhat different lines from those taken here. See "Justice
as Fairness," *Philosophical Review* LXVII (1958), pp. 164-94.
[38] *Op. cit.*, p. 47. Cf. pp. 16f.

sense transcend both the feelings of the speaker and the institutions of human society—principles which are claimed to be absolutely or eternally valid in the sense at least that all men or an impartial spectator, taking the appropriate point of view and being free and fully informed (God would be such a spectator), would accept them. T. D. Weldon partly sees this when he says,

> "They haven't really any right . . ." suggests that there is some absolute standard by which actual legislation can be appraised and criticized . . . The illusion here arises because most of us have been trained to talk as if there were a Grand Appraiser who knows all the right answers and to whose Appraisals we try to approach.[39]

Weldon wants us to shake off the illusion, but this is to miss the point at least as much as Brunner does. Even if we seek to make our appraisals on empirical grounds, as Weldon advocates, we will nevertheless be claiming that they are such appraisals as anyone would agree to who had made enquiry and knew all the empirical facts. The point is that when we judge that something is good, true, beautiful, or just, we always purport to be taking a certain public point of view and claim that our judgment will be sustained by anyone who is free and enlightened and takes that point of view. In this sense Brunner, not Weldon, is right—and so was Tennyson when he said:

> The good, the true, the pure, the just—
> Take the charm "Forever" from them, and
> they crumble into dust.

For, in this sense, the quest for social justice, though it is carried on in time, is carried on under the aspect of eternity.

[39] *The Vocabulary of Politics* (London: Penguin Books, 1953), pp. 58, 170.

Justice and
Equality

GREGORY VLASTOS

I

The close connection between justice and equality is manifest in both history and language. The great historic struggles for social justice have centered about some demand for equal rights: the struggle against slavery, political absolutism, economic exploitation, the disfranchisement of the lower and middle classes and the disfranchisement of women, colonialism, racial oppression. On the linguistic side let me mention a curiosity that will lead us into the thick of our problem. When Aristotle in Book V of the *Nicomachean Ethics* comes to grips with distributive justice, almost the first remark he has to make is that "justice is equality, as all men believe it to be, quite apart from any argument." [1] And well they might if they are Greeks, for their ordinary word for equality, *to ison* or *isotes,* comes closer to being the right word for "justice" than does the word *dikaiosyne,* which we usually translate as "justice." [2] Thus, when a man speaks Greek he will be likely to say "equality" and

---

[1] 1131a 13.

[2] "Righteousness," the quality of acting rightly, would be closer to the sense of *dikaiosyne:* at *Nicomachean Ethics* 1129b 27ff., Aristotle finds it necessary to explain that, though his theme is *dikaiosyne,* he will not be discussing "virtue entire" or "complete virtue in its fullest sense." No one writing an essay on *justice* would find any need to offer this kind of explanation; nor would he be tempted, regardless of his theory of justice, to offer (as Plato does at *Rep.* 433ab) "performing the function(s) for which one's nature is best fitted" as a *definition* of "justice."

31

mean "justice." But it so happens that Aristotle, like Plato and others before him, believed firmly that a just distribution is in general an unequal one.[3] And to say this, if "equal" is your word for "just," you would have to say that an "equal" distribution is an *unequal* one. A way had been found to hold this acrobatic linguistic posture by saying that in this connection *isotes* meant "geometrical equality," i.e., proportionality; hence the "equal" (just, fair) distribution to persons of unequal merit would have to be unequal. This tour de force must have provoked many an honest man at the time as much as it has enraged Professor Popper[4] in ours. We may view it more dispassionately as classical testimony to the strength of the tie between equality and justice: even those who meant to break the conceptual link could not, or would not, break the verbal one. The meritarian view of justice paid reluctant homage to the equalitarian one by using the vocabulary of equality to assert the justice of inequality.

But when the equalitarian has drawn from this what comfort he may, he still has to face the fact that the expropriation of his word "equality" could be carried through so reputably and so successfully that its remote inheritance has made it possible for us to speak now in a perfectly matter of fact way of "equitable inequalities" or "inequitable equalities." This kind of success cannot be wholly due to the tactical skill of those who carried out the original maneuver; though one may envy the virtuosity with which Plato disposes of the whole notion of democratic equality in a single sentence (or rather less, a participial clause) when he speaks of democracy as "distributing an odd sort of equality to equals and unequals."[5] The democrats themselves would have been intellectually defenseless against that

---

[3] Plato, *Gorgias* 508a (and E. R. Dodds *ad loc.* in Plato, *Gorgias* [Oxford, 1959]); *Rep.* 558c; *Laws* 744bc, 757a ff. Isocrates, *Areopagiticus* 21-22; *To Nicocles* 14. *Aristotle, Nic. Eth.* 1131a 15ff., and the commentary by F. Dirlmeier, *Aristoteles, Nikomachische Ethik* (Berlin, 1956), pp. 404-407.

[4] K. R. Popper, *The Open Society and its Enemies* (London, 1949), pp. 79-80. "Why did Plato claim that justice meant inequality if, in general usage, it meant equality? To me the only likely reply seems to be that he wanted to make propaganda for his totalitarian state by persuading the people that it was the 'just' state." He adds shortly after: "His attack on equalitarianism was not an honest attack," p. 80.

[5] *Rep.* 558c; and cf. *Laws* 757a: "For when equality is given to unequals the result is inequality, unless due measure is applied."

quip. Their faith in democracy had no deep roots in any concept of human equality; the *isonomia* (equality of law) on which they prided themselves was the club-privilege of those who had had the good judgment to pick their ancestors from free Athenian stock of the required purity of blood. But even if we could imagine a precocious humanitarian in or before Plato's time, founding the rights of the citizen on the rights of man, it is not clear that even he would be proof against Plato's criticism. For what Plato would like to know is whether his equalitarian opponent really means to universalize equality: would he, would anyone, wish to say that there are no just inequalities? That there are no rights in respect of which men are unequal?

One would think that this would be among the first questions that would occur to equalitarians, and would have had long since a clear and firm answer. Strange as it may seem, this has not happened. The question has been largely evaded. Let me give an example: Article I of the Declaration of Rights of Man and Citizen (enacted by the Constituent Assembly of the First French Republic in 1791) reads: "Men are born and remain free and equal in rights. Social distinctions can be based only upon public utility." Bentham takes the first sentence to mean that men are equal in *all* rights.[6] One would like to think that this was a wilful misunderstanding. For it would be only too obvious to the drafters of the Declaration that those "social distinctions" of which they go on to speak would entail many inequalities of right. Thus the holder of a unique political office (say, the president of a republic) would not be equal in all rights to all other men or even to one other man: no other man would have equal right to this office, or to as high an office; and many would not have equal right to any political office, even if they had, as they would according to the republican constitution, equal right of eligibility to all offices. But if this is in the writers' minds, why don't they come out and say that men are born and remain

[6] He assumes it entails that, e.g., "the rights of the heir of the most indigent family (are) equal to the rights of the heir of the most wealthy," the rights of the apprentice equal to those of his master, those of the madman and the idiot equal to those of the sane, and so forth. "A Critical Examination of the Declaration of Rights," in *Anarchical Fallacies*. In *Works* (London, 1843), ed. John Bowring, Vol. II, pp. 489ff., at p. 498.

equal in some rights, but are either not born or do not remain equal
in a great many others? They act as though they were afraid to say
the latter on this excessively public occasion, lest their public con-
strue the admission of some unequal rights as out of harmony with
the ringing commitment to human rights which is the keynote of the
Declaration. What is this? Squeamishness? Confusion? Something of
both? Or has it perhaps a sound foundation and, if so, in what?
Plato's question is not answered. It is allowed to go by default.

There is here, as so often in the tradition of natural rights, a lack
of definiteness which is exasperating to those who look for plain
and consecutive thinking in moral philosophy. Coming back to
this tradition fresh from the systems of Plato or Hobbes or Hume,
with their clean, functional lines, one feels that whether or not the
case for inequality has ever been proved, it has at least been made
clear from both the aristocratic and the utilitarian side; while
the case for equality, housed in the rambling and somewhat rundown
mansion of natural rights, has fared so poorly that when one puts
a question like the one I just raised, one can't be sure of what the
answer is, or even that there is supposed to be one. And much the
same is true of several other questions that remain after one has
completely cut out one earlier source of confusion: the mythological
prehistory of a supposed state of nature. Taking "natural rights"
to mean simply *human* rights—that is to say, rights which are human
not in the trivial sense that those who have them are men, but in
the challenging sense that in order to have them they need only be
men—one would still like to know:

(1) What is the range of these rights? The French Declaration
states: "these rights are liberty, property, security, and resistance
to oppression." The imprudent beginning—"these rights are"
instead of Jefferson's more cautious, "among these rights are"—
makes it look as though the four natural rights named here are
meant to be all the rights there are. If so, what happened to the
pursuit of happiness? Is that the same as liberty? As for property,
this was not a natural right before Locke,[7] and not always after him,

[7] Locke's argument that property is a natural right is a momentous innovation,
"a landmark in the history of thought." O. Giercke, *Natural Law and the
Theory of Society 1500 to 1800* (Cambridge: Cambridge Univ. Press, 1950), p. 103.
But this is not to say that, if one looks hard enough, one will not find anticipa-

e.g., not for Jefferson.[8] And what of welfare rights? They are not mentioned in the French document, nor are they implied by "security."

(2) Can the doctrine of natural rights find a place for each of the following well-known maxims of distributive justice:

1. To each according to his *need*.
2. To each according to his *worth*.
3. To each according to his *merit*.
4. To each according to his *work*.[9]

And we might add a fifth which does not seem to have worked its way to the same level of adage-like respectability, but has as good a claim as some of the others:

5. To each according to the *agreements* he has made.

By making judicious selections from this list one can "justicize" [10] extreme inequalities of distribution. It is thus that Plato concludes that the man who can no longer work has lost his right to live,[11] and Bentham that no just limits can be set to the terms on which labor can be bought, used, and used up.[12] Hobbes, most frugal of moral philosophers, operates with just the last of these maxims;[13] making the keeping of covenants the defining element of justice, he

---

tions of Locke's theory. See E. S. Corwin, *The "Higher Law" Background of American Constitutional Law*, Great Seal Books edition (Ithaca: Cornell Univ. Press, 1955), p. 61, note 60; J. W. Gough, *Locke's Political Philosophy* (New York: Oxford Univ. Press, 1950, p. 80). (For some of these references, and for other useful suggestions, I am indebted to Dr. Hugo Bedau.)

[8] See, e.g., Ursula M. von Eckardt, *The Pursuit of Happiness in the Democratic Creed* (New York: Frederick A. Praeger, 1959), pp. 103-08.

[9] For a similar enumeration see Charles Perelman, *De la Justice* (Brussels, 1945).

[10] Cf. Frankena, *supra* p. 5.

[11] *Rep.* 406e-407a.

[12] "When the question of slavery is not considered there is little to say respecting the conditions of master and its correlative conditions, constituted by the different kinds of servants. All these conditions are the effects of contract; these contracts the parties interested may arrange to suit themselves," *Principles of the Civil Code.* In *Works*, Bowring, ed., vol. 1, p. 341.

[13] The fifth: "the definition of *Injustice* is no other than *the not performance of covenant.* And whatsoever is not unjust is just." *Leviathan*, Part I, Ch. 15.

decimates civil liberties *more geometrico*.[14] These premises were not, of course, the only ones from which such morally dismal results were reached by these clear-headed and upright men; but they were the controlling ones. If merit or work or agreement, or any combination of the three, are made the final principles of distributive justice, it will not be hard to find plausible collateral premises from which to get such results. What then should a natural rights philosopher do with these maxims? Must he regard them as fifth-columnists? Or can he keep them as members of his working team, useful, if subordinate, principles of his equalitarian justice? Can this be done without making concessions to inequality which will divide his allegiance to equality?

(3) Finally, are natural rights "absolute," i.e., are their claims unexceptionable. If I have a natural right to a given benefit does it follow that I ought to be granted that benefit in all possible circumstances no matter how my other rights or those of others might be affected? Is this the meaning of the well-known statements that natural rights are "inalienable" and "imprescriptible"?

I believe that all these questions admit of reasonable answers which, when worked out fully, would amount to a revised theory of natural rights or, what is the same thing, a theory of human rights: I shall use the two expressions interchangeably. Progress has been made in this direction in recent years in a number of important essays.[15] I shall borrow freely results reached by various contributors

[14] That "nothing the sovereign representative can do to a subject, on what pretense soever, can properly be called injustice or injury" (*op. cit.*, Part II, Ch. 21) is presented as a logical consequence of (a) every subject is the "author" of each act of his sovereign and (b) no man can be the author of injustice or injury to himself. (a) follows from the definitions of "sovereign" and "subject," Part I, Ch. 18.

[15] The ones to which I am most indebted are: R. B. Perry, *Puritanism and Democracy* (New York: Vanguard Press, 1944) pp. 446ff.; Margaret Macdonald, "Natural Rights," *Proc. Aristotelian Society*, 1947-48 (reprinted in P. Laslett, *Philosophy, Politics and Society* [Oxford: Blackwell, 1956]); A. I. Melden and W. K. Frankena, "Human Rights," in *Science, Language and Human Rights* (Philadelphia, 1952); the symposium on "Are There Natural Rights?" by H. L. A. Hart, S. M. Brown, and Frankena in *Philosophical Review* 64 (1955); R. Wollheim, "Equality and Equal Rights," *Proc. Aristotelian Society*, 1955-56 (reprinted in F. A. Olafson, *Justice and Social Policy* [Englewood Cliffs, N. J.: Prentice-Hall, 1961]); R. Brandt, *Ethical Theory* (Englewood Cliffs, N. J.: Prentice-Hall, 1959) Ch. 17; A. I. Melden, *Rights and Right Conduct* (Oxford: Blackwell, 1959); and

to this work, though without taking time to make explicit acknowledgments or register specific disagreements.

Let me begin with the answer to the third of the questions I raised. Are human rights absolute? All of these writers would say, "No." I am convinced that in this they are right,[16] and am even prepared to add that neither is there anything explicitly contrary to this in that branch of the classical theory which is of greatest interest to us today: in Locke, for example.[17] Locke has indeed been understood to mean that natural rights are absolute.[18] But nowhere does Locke *say* this. Contrariwise he believes many things which imply the opposite. For example, he would certainly approve of imprisonment as a punishment for crime; and we hear him recommending that beggars be detained in houses of correction or impressed in the navy.[19] Such constraints he would have to reckon justified exceptions to that freedom of movement which all persons claim in virtue of their natural right to liberty. So too he would have to think of the death penalty for convicted criminals, or of a military order which would bring death to many of those obeying it, as justified exceptions to some men's natural right to life. Even the right to property—indeed, that special form of it which is upheld more zealously than any other right in the *Second Treatise,* one's right not to be deprived of property without consent[20]—could not be unconditional; Locke would have to concede that it should be over-ruled, e.g., in a famine when stores of hoarded food are requisitioned by public authority. We would, therefore, improve the con-

---

cf. H. L. A. Hart, *The Concept of Law* (New York: Oxford Univ. Press, 1961), Ch. IX, "Laws and Morals."

[16] For this I am especially indebted to discussion with Richard Brandt.

[17] Nor in the Thomist version as interpreted by J. Maritain. See his distinction between the "possession" and the "exercise" of a natural right (unexceptionable and exceptionable, respectively), *Man and the State* (Chicago: Univ. of Chicago Press, 1951), pp. 101-03.

[18] E.g., E. F. Carritt, *Ethical and Political Thinking* (Oxford: Oxford Univ. Press, 1947), pp. 154ff. Brandt, *op. cit.,* p. 442. No text is cited from Locke to support this very widespread interpretation. Such statements as "the obligations of the law of nature cease not in society," *Second Treatise of Government,* 135, are too general to determine the point at issue here.

[19] See his proposals for the reform of the Poor Law submitted to the Board of Trade in 1697: H. R. Fox-Bourne, *Life of Locke* (London, 1876), vol. 2, pp. 379-81.

[20] 138, 139. Cf. other references in J. W. Gough, *op. cit.,* p. 85, Note 1.

sistency of Locke's theory if we understood him to mean that natural rights are subject to justified exceptions.[21] In any case, I shall adhere to his view here and, borrowing from current usage, shall speak of human rights as "prima facie" rights[22] to mean that the claims of any of them may be over-ruled in special circumstances.[23] Can one say this without giving away the radical difference which the traditional doctrine fixed between natural rights and all others? To this the answer would be that, though in this respect all rights are alike, the vital difference remains untouched: one need only be a man to have *prima facie* rights to life, liberty, welfare, and the like; but to be a man is not all one needs to have a *prima facie* right to the house he happens to own or the job he happens to hold. As for the "inalienability" and "imprescriptibility" of natural rights, we may understand them with this proviso to mean exactly what they say: that no man can alienate (i.e., sign away, transfer by contract)[24] a *prima facie* natural right, his own or anyone else's; and that no people can lose *prima facie* natural rights by prescription, e.g., in virtue of the

[21] Admitting that to do this is to add something of substance to his own explicit doctrine. He himself never refers to cases such as those I have mentioned as exceptions to natural rights.

[22] See Frankena, "Human Rights" (fn. 15 above), p. 127, and "Are There Natural Rights?" pp. 228ff.; Brandt, *op. cit.*, pp. 441ff. For some objections to this usage see Sir David Ross, *The Right and the Good* (Oxford: Oxford Univ. Press, 1939), p. 20; for strong opposition, Melden, *Rights and Right Conduct*, pp. 18ff. I am not entirely happy with this usage, but neither can I propose a better. Part of the objection is met by the clarification in the following note.

[23] Given "right" = "justified claim" (Oxford English Dictionary), *prima facie* qualifies "justified." A *prima facie* right is one whose claim has *prima facie* justification, i.e., *is* justified, unless there are stronger counter-claims in the particular situation in which it is made, the burden of proof resting always on the counter-claims. "Claim" here has a much broader sense than "asserted claim"; it is related to "claiming" in much the same way as "proposition" to "propounding"; it is something which may be claimed, as a proposition is something which may be propounded. To say that a right is a justified claim is to say that it is something which could be claimed with justification, i.e., a claim which others have the obligation to grant if (but not, only if) it is asserted.

[24] The normal sense of "alienate" when applied to rights in legal, or quasi-legal, contexts. To defend the inalienability (though without using this word) of one's right to be free from subjection to the arbitrary will of another, Locke thinks it sufficient to argue that one cannot forfeit this right "by compact or his own consent," *Second Treatise*, 23, and cannot "transfer to another" (135) this right by a voluntary act.

time-hallowed possession of despotic power over them by a royal dynasty.[25]

Does this entirely allay our misgivings? It does not, and it should not. To say that a natural right is a *prima facie* right is to say that there are cases in which it is perfectly just to disallow its claim; and unless we have definite assurance as to the limits within which this may occur, we have no way of telling whether we are better off with this *prima facie* right than we would be without it. If *anything* may count as an allowable exception, then what does the right give us that we would otherwise lack? If only some things are to count, we need to know what sort of things these are to be, in order to know what, if anything, our right is worth. Richard Brandt does give us some such information. He implies that only for *moral* reasons will the exceptions be allowed.[26] This tells us something, but not enough. How can we know that moral reasons will not be forthcoming to nullify the efficacy of the natural right? From William Frankena's remarks we get something stronger: to "justicize" an exception we may adduce only considerations of justice ("just-making" ones).[27] This is better, but still not enough. What we ought to know is whether the considerations of justice which allow us to make exceptions to a natural right in special circumstances are the same considerations which require us to uphold it in general. For if we are to have two sets of "just-making" reasons, one set requiring us to uphold these rights, the other permitting us to over-rule them, we shall be in a state of moral uncertainty and anxiety about our natural rights, and our condition will not be improved if we label it with Professor Gallie "moral polyarchy." [28]

[25] For the relevant sense of "prescription," see the *Shorter Oxford English Dictionary*, s.v., II (b): "uninterrupted use or possession from time immemorial, or for a period fixed by law as giving a title or right; hence title or right acquired by such use or possession." On prescription as the foundation of rights of government and property see, e.g., Edmund Burke: "Our constitution is a prescriptive constitution; it is a constitution whose sole authority is that it has existed time out of mind. . . . Prescription is the most solid of all titles, not only to property, but, which is to secure that property, to government," Reform of Representation in the House of Commons (1782), *Works*, Vol. 6.

[26] *Op. cit.*, pp. 410 and 446.

[27] *Supra*, p. 10ff.

[28] W. B. Gallie, "Liberal Morality and Socialist Morality," in Laslett (*op. cit.*, in n. 15 above), pp. 116ff. Each of us, in his view, is "internally divided, pulled

We must find *reasons for our natural rights which will be the only moral reasons for just exceptions* to them in special circumstances.

This may look like a predictably unfulfillable demand, for it seems self-contradictory. But it is certainly not the latter. There is nothing self-contradictory about saying that reasons requiring a general pattern of action may permit, or even require, a departure from it in special circumstances. Thus my reasons for eating three meals a day are, say, pleasure and physical need; for these same reasons I might eat on special occasions four or five meals in a single day, or two or one. The analogy is not perfect, but it does give a rough idea of the lines along which we may concede justified exceptions to natural rights without jeopardizing the fundamental place they must hold in our scheme of justice, if we are to keep them there at all. And since all of them are equal rights (i.e., rights to equal treatment), a parallel observation may be made about the problem with which we started: An equalitarian concept of justice may admit just inequalities without inconsistency if, and only if, it provides grounds for equal human rights *which are also grounds for unequal rights of other sorts*. Such grounds, if we could find them, should carry right through all five of the maxims of distributive justice I listed above, showing how these maxims can be tied together as principles of justice and of the same concept of justice. I propose to identify these grounds in Section II, and then show, in Section IV, how on these grounds, supplemented by certain factual considerations, inequalities of merit may be recognized by the theory of equalitarian justice which I will expound in Section III.

II

Let me begin with the first on my list of maxims of distributive justice: "To each according to his need." Since needs are often unequal, this looks like a precept of unequal distribution. But this is wrong. It is in fact *the most perfect form of equal distribution*. To explain this let me take one of the best established rights in the natural law tradition: the right to the security of life and person.

---

this way and that on different issues by the claims and counter-claims of two conflicting moralities" (p. 121), each of which has its "own autonomous, i.e., not mutually corrigible, aims and standards" (p. 132).

Believing that this is an equal right, what do we feel this means in cases of special need?

Suppose, for instance, New Yorker X gets a note from Murder, Inc., that looks like business. To allocate several policemen and plainclothesmen to guard him over the next few weeks at a cost a hundred times greater than the per capita cost of security services to other citizens during the same period, is surely *not* to make an exception to the equal distribution required by the equal right of all citizens to the security of their life and person; it is not done on the assumption that X has a greater right to security or a right to greater security. If the visitor from Mars drew this conclusion from the behavior of the police, he would be told that he was just mistaken. The greater allocation of community resources in X's favor, we would have to explain, is made precisely *because* X's security rights are equal to those of other people in New York. This means that X is entitled to the same level of police-made security as is maintained for other New Yorkers. Hence in these special circumstances, where his security level would drop to zero without extra support, he should be given this to bring his security level nearer the normal. I say "nearer," not "up to" the normal, because I am talking of New York as of 1961. If I were thinking of New York with an ideal municipal government, ideally supplied with police resources, I *would* say "up to the normal," because that is what equality of right would ideally mean. But as things are, perhaps the best that can be done for X without disrupting the general level of security maintained for all the other New Yorkers is to decrease his chances of being bumped off in a given week to, say, one to ten thousand, while those of ordinary citizens, with ordinary protection are, say, one to ten million—no small difference.[29] Now if New York were more affluent, it would be able to buy more equality[30] of security for its

---

[29] These figures, needless to say, are "pulled out of a hat."

[30] This point was first suggested to me by Professor Kenneth Boulding's striking remark that "only a rich society can afford to be equalitarian," *The Economics of Peace* (Englewood Cliffs, N. J.: Prentice-Hall, 1945), p. 111. The more guarded form in which I am stating the point will protect it against apparent counter-examples to Boulding's remark, e.g., the astonishing equalitarianism that was still practiced by the Eskimos of the Coronation Gulf and the Mackenzie River early in this century (see V. Stefansson's essay in *Freedom*, Ruth N. Anshen, ed., [New York: Harcourt, Brace and World, 1940]).

citizens (as well as more security): by getting more, and perhaps also better paid, policemen, it would be able to close the gap between security maintained for people in ordinary circumstances and that supplied in cases of special need, like that of X in his present jam. Here we stumble on something of considerable interest: that approximation to the goal of completely equal security benefits for all citizens is a function of two variables: first, and quite obviously, of the pattern of distribution of the resources; second, and less obviously, of their size. If the distributable resources are so meager that they are all used up to maintain a general level barely sufficient for ordinary needs, their reallocation to meet exceptional need will look too much like robbing Peter to pay Paul. In such conditions there is likely to be little, if any, provision for extremity of need and, what is more, the failure to meet the extremity will not be felt as a social injustice but as a calamity of fate. And since humanity has lived most of its life under conditions of general indigence, we can understand why it has been so slow to connect provision for special need with the notion of justice, and has so often made it a matter of charity; and why "to each according to his need" did not become popularized as a precept of justice until the first giant increase in the productive resources, and then only by men like Blanc and Marx, who projected an image of a super-affluent, machine-run society on the grid of an austerely equalitarian conception of justice.[31]

So we can see why distribution according to personal need, far from conflicting with the equality of distribution required by a human right, is so linked with its very meaning that under ideal conditions equality of right would coincide with distribution according to personal need. Our visitor misunderstood the sudden mobilization of New York policemen in favor of Mr. X, because he failed to understand that it is benefits to persons, not allocation of resources as such, that are meant to be made equal; for then he

[31] The well-known maxim, "from each according to his ability, to each according to his need" (Karl Marx, *Critique of the Gotha Programme,* 1875), echoes, without acknowledgment, a remark in the 9th edition of Louis Blanc's *L'Organization du travail* (Paris, 1850) that "true equality" is that "which apportions work to ability and recompense to needs" (cited in D. O. Wagner, *Social Reformers* [New York: The Macmillan Co., 1946], p. 248).

would have seen at once that unequal distribution of resources would be required to equalize benefits in cases of unequal need. But if he saw this he might then ask, "But why do you want this sort of equality?" My answer would have to be: Because the human worth of all persons is equal, however unequal may be their merit. To the explanation of this proposition I shall devote the balance of this Section.

By "merit" I shall refer throughout this essay to all the kinds of valuable qualities or performances in respect of which persons may be graded.[32] The concept will not be restricted to moral actions or dispositions.[33] Thus wit, grace of manner, and technical skill count as meritorious qualities fully as much as sincerity, generosity, or courage. Any valuable human characteristic, or cluster of characteristics, will qualify, provided only it is "acquired," i.e., represents what its possessor has himself made of his natural endowments and environmental opportunities. Given the immense variety of individual differences, it will be commonly the case that of any two persons either may excel the other in respect of different kinds or sub-kinds of merit. Thus if A and B are both clever and brave men, A may be much the cleverer as a business man, B as a literary critic, and A may excel in physical, B in moral, courage. It should be clear from just this that to speak of "a person's merit" will be strictly senseless except insofar as this is an elliptical way of referring to that person's merits, i.e., to those specifiable qualities or activities in which he rates well. So if there is a value attaching to the person himself as an integral and unique individual, *this* value will not fall under merit or be reducible to it. For it is of the essence of merit, as here defined, to be a grading concept; and there is no way of grading individuals as such. We can only grade them with respect to their qualities, hence only by abstracting from their individuality.

---

[32] This is only one of the senses recognized by the dictionary (*The Shorter Oxford English Dictionary*, s.v., 4 and 6): "Excellence," "An Excellence," the latter being illustrated by "Would you ask for his merits? Alas! he has none" (from Goldsmith). In the other senses listed by the dictionary the word either *means* "desert" or at least includes this in its meaning. On the present use of "merit" the connection with "desert" is synthetic.

[33] As is done by some philosophical moralists, e.g., Sir David Ross, *op. cit.*, pp. 135ff., where "merit" and (moral) "virtue" are co-extensive.

If *A* is valued for some meritorious quality, *m*, his individuality does not enter into the valuation. As an individual he is then dispensable; his place could be taken without loss of value by any other individual with as good an *m*-rating. Nor would matters change by multiplying and diversifying the meritorious qualities with which *A* is endowed. No matter how enviable a package of well-rounded excellence *A* may represent, it would still follow that, if he is valued only for his merit, he is not being valued as an individual. To be sure individuals *may* be valued only for their merits. This happens all too commonly. *A* might be valued in just this way by *P,* the president of his company, for whom *A,* highly successful vice-president in charge of sales, amusing dinner-guest, and fine asset to the golf club, is simply high-grade equipment in various complexes of social machinery which *P* controls or patronizes. On the other hand, it is possible that, much as *P* prizes this conjunct of qualities (*M*), he values *A* also as an individual. *A* may be his son, and he may be genuinely fond of him. If so, his affection will be for *A,* not for his *M*-qualities. The latter *P* approves, admires, takes pride in, and the like. But his affection and good will are for *A,* and *not only because,* or *insofar as,* *A* has the *M*-qualities. For *P* may be equally fond of another son who rates well below *A* in *P*'s scoring system. Moreover, *P*'s affection for *A,* as distinct from his approval or admiration of him, need not fluctuate with the ups and downs in *A*'s achievements. Perhaps *A* had some bad years after graduating from college, and it looked then as though his brilliant gifts would be wasted. It does not follow that *P*'s love for *A* then lapsed or even ebbed. Constancy of affection in the face of variations of merit is one of the surest tests of whether or not a parent does love a child. If he feels fond of it only when it performs well, and turns coldly indifferent or hostile when its achievements slump, then his feeling for the child can scarcely be called *love.* There are many relations in which one's liking or esteem for a person are strictly conditional on his measuring up to certain standards. But convincing evidence that the relation is of this type is no evidence that the relation is one of parental love or any other kind of love. It does nothing to show that one has this feeling, or any feeling, for an *individual,*

rather than for a place-holder of qualities one likes to see instanti-
ated by somebody or other close about one.

Now if this concept of value attaching to a person's individual
existence, over and above his merit—"individual worth," [34] let me
call it—were applicable *only* in relations of personal love, it would
be irrelevant for the analysis of justice. To serve our purpose its
range of application must be coextensive with that of justice. It
must hold in all human relations, including (or rather, especially in)
the most impersonal of all, those to total strangers, fellow-citizens
or fellow-men. I must show that the concept of individual worth
does meet this condition.

Consider its role in our political community, taking the prescriptions of our laws for the treatment of persons as the index to our
valuations. For merit (among other reasons) persons may be ap-
pointed or elected to public office or given employment by state
agencies. For demerit they may lose licences, jobs, offices; they may
be fined, jailed, or even put to death. But in a large variety of
law-regulated actions directed to individuals, either by private
persons or by organs of the state, the question of merit and demerit
does not arise. The "equal protection of the laws" is due to persons
not to meritorious ones, or to them in some degree above others.[35]
So too for the right to vote. One does not have it for being intelligent
and public-spirited, or lose it for being lazy, ignorant, or viciously
selfish. One is entitled to exercise it as long as, having registered, one
manages to keep out of jail. This kind of arrangement would look
like whimsy or worse, like sheer immoralism, if the only values
recognized in our political community were those of merit. For
obviously there is nothing compulsory about our political system;
we could certainly devise, if we so wished, workable alternatives

[34] That this is *intrinsic* worth goes without saying. But I do not put this term
into my label, since I want to distinguish this kind of value as sharply as possible
from that of merit, and I include under "merit" not only extrinsically, but also
intrinsically, valuable qualities.

[35] A modicum of merit by way of self-help and law-obedience is generally presupposed. But it would be a mistake to think of the protection of the laws as a
reward for good behavior. Thus many legal protections are due as much to
those who will not look out for themselves as to those who do, and to law-
breakers as much as to law-observers.

which would condition fundamental rights on certain kinds of merit. For example, we might have three categories of citizenship. The top one might be for those who meet high educational qualifications and give definite evidence of responsible civic interest, e.g., by active participation in political functions, tenure of public office, record of leadership in civic organizations and support to them, and the like. People in this *A*-category might have multiple votes in all elections and exclusive eligibility for the more important political offices; they might also be entitled to a higher level of protection by the police and to a variety of other privileges and immunities. At the other end there would be a *C*-category, disfranchised and legally underprivileged, for those who do not meet some lower educational test or have had a record of law-infraction or have been on the relief rolls for over three months. In between would be the *B*'s with ordinary suffrage and intermediate legal status.

This "*M*-system" would be more complicated and cumbersome than ours. But something like it could certainly be made to work if we were enamoured of its peculiar scheme of values. Putting aside the question of efficiency, it gives us a picture of a community whose political valuations, conceived entirely in terms of merit, would never be grounded on individual worth, so that this notion would there be politically useless.[36] For us, on the other hand, it is indispensable.[37] We have to appeal to it when we try to make sense of the fact that our legal system accords to all citizens an identical status, carrying with it rights such as the *M*-system reserves to the *B*'s or the *A*'s, and some of which (like suffrage or freedom of speech) have been denied even to the nobility in some caste-systems of the past. This last comparison is worth pressing: it brings out the illuminating fact that in one fundamental respect our society is much more like a caste society (with a *unique* caste) than like the *M*-system. The latter has no place for a rank of dignity which descends on an individual by the purely existential circumstance (the "accident") of birth and remains his unalterably for life. To

---

[36] Though it might have uses in the family or other relations.

[37] Even where a purely pragmatic justification is offered for democracy (e.g., Pendleton Herring, *Politics of Democracy* [New York: W. W. Norton & Co., 1940]) equality of worth must still be acknowledged, if only as a popular "myth" or "dogma."

reproduce this feature of our system we would have to look not only to caste-societies, but to extremely rigid ones, since most of them make some provision for elevation in rank for rare merit or degradation for extreme demerit. In our legal system no such thing can happen: even a criminal may not be sentenced to second-class citizenship.[38] And the fact that first-class citizenship, having been made common, is no longer a mark of distinction does not trivialize the privileges it entails. It is the simple truth, not declamation, to speak of it, as I have done, as a "rank of dignity" in some ways comparable to that enjoyed by hereditary nobilities of the past. To see this one need only think of the position of groups in our society who have been cheated out of this status by the subversion of their constitutional rights. The difference in social position between Negroes and whites described in Dollard's classic[39] is not smaller than that between, say, bourgeoisie and aristocracy in the *ancien régime* of France. It might well be greater.

Consider finally the role of the same value in the moral community. Here differences of merit are so conspicuous and pervasive that we might even be tempted to *define* the moral response to a person in terms of moral approval or disapproval of his acts or disposition, i.e., in terms of the response to his moral merit. But there are many kinds of moral response for which a person's merit is as irrelevant as is that of New Yorker X when he appeals to the police for help. If I see someone in danger of drowning I will not need to satisfy myself about his moral character before going to his aid. I owe assistance to any man in such circumstances, not merely to good men. Nor is it only in rare and exceptional cases, as this example might suggest, that my obligations to others are independent of their moral merit. To be sincere, reliable, fair, kind, tolerant, unintrusive, modest in my relations with my fellows is not due them because they have made brilliant or even passing moral grades, but simply because they happen to be fellow-members of the moral community.

[38] No one, I trust, will confuse second-class citizenship with extreme punishments, such as the death-penalty or a life-sentence, or, for that matter, with *any* legal punishment in a democratic society. Second-class citizens are those deprived of rights without any presumption of legal guilt.

[39] John Dollard, *Caste and Class in a Southern Town* (New Haven: Yale Univ. Press, 1937).

It is not necessary to add, "members in good standing." The moral community is not a club from which members may be dropped for delinquency. Our morality does not provide for moral outcasts or half-castes. It does provide for punishment. But this takes place *within* the moral community and under its rules. It is for this reason that, for example, one has no right to be cruel to a cruel person. His offense against the moral law has not put him outside the law. He is still protected by its prohibition of cruelty—as much so as are kind persons. The pain inflicted on him as punishment for his offense does not close out the reserve of good will on the part of all others which is his birthright as a human being; it is a limited withdrawal from it. Capital punishment, if we believe in it, is no exception. The fact that a man has been condemned to death does not license his jailors to beat him or virtuous citizens to lynch him.

Here, then, as in the single-status political community, we acknowledge personal rights which are not proportioned to merit and could not be justified by merit. Their only justification could be the value which persons have simply because they are persons: their "intrinsic value as individual human beings," as Frankena calls it; the "infinite value" or the "sacredness" of their individuality, as others have called it. I shall speak of it as "individual human worth"; or "human worth," for short. What these expressions stand for is also expressed by saying that men are "ends in themselves." This latter concept is Kant's. Some of the kinks in his formulation of it[40] can be straightened out by explaining it as follows: Everything other than a person can only have value *for* a person. This applies not only to physical objects, natural or manmade, which have only instrumental value, but also to those products of the human spirit which have also intrinsic, no less than extrinsic, value: an epic poem, a scientific theory, a legal system, a moral

---

[40] See, e.g., H. Sidgwick, *Methods of Ethics* (London, 1874), p. 363. For a parallel objection see the next note. Still another is that Kant, using the notion of *intrinsic worth* (*Würde* in contrast to *Preis*) to define *end in itself*, and hence as its sufficient condition, tends to conflate the value of *persons* as ends in themselves with that of their *moral merit*. Thus, though he says that "Respect [the attitude due to a being which is an end in itself] always applies to persons only" (*Critique of Practical Reason*, trans. L. W. Beck [New York, 1956], p. 79) he illustrates by respect for a person's "righteousness" (*l.c.*) and remarks: "Respect is a tribute we cannot refuse to pay to merit . . ." (p. 80).

disposition. Even such things as these will have value only because they can be (a) experienced or felt to be valuable by human beings and (b) chosen by them from competing alternatives. Thus of everything without exception it will be true to say: if x is valuable and is not a person, then x will have value for some individual other than itself. Hence even a musical composition or a courageous deed, valued for their own sake, as "ends" not as means to anything else, will still fall into an entirely different category from that of the *valuers,* who do not need to be valued as "ends" by someone else[41] in order to have value. In just this sense persons, and only persons, are "ends in themselves."

The two factors in terms of which I have described the value of the valuer—the capacities answering to (a) and (b) above—may not be exhaustive. But their conjunction offers a translation of "individual human worth" whose usefulness for working purposes will speak for itself. To (a) I might refer as "happiness," if I could use this term as Plato and Aristotle used *eudaimonia,* i.e., without the exclusively hedonistic connotations which have since been clamped on it. It will be less misleading to use "well-being" or "welfare" for what I intend here; that is, the enjoyment of value in all the forms in which it can be experienced by human beings. To (b) I shall refer as "freedom," bringing under this term not only conscious choices and deliberate decisions but also those subtler modulations and more spontaneous expressions of individual preference which could scarcely be called "choices" or "decisions" without some forcing of language. So understood, a person's well-being and freedom are aspects of his individual existence as unique and unrepeatable as is that existence itself: If A and B are listening to the same symphony with similar tastes and dispositions, we may speak of their enjoying the "same" good, or having the "same" enjoyment, and say that each has made the "same" choice for this way of spending his time and money. But here "same" will mean no more than "very similar"; the two enjoyments and choices, occurring in the consciousness of A

---

[41] Though, of course, they may be (if they are loved or respected as persons). In that case it will not be, strictly, the persons, but their welfare or freedom, which will be the "end" of those who so love or respect them: since only that which can be realized by action can be an end, to speak of another *person* as my end is bad logical grammar.

and *B* respectively, are absolutely unique. So in translating *"A's human worth"* into "the worth of *A*'s well-being and freedom" we are certainly meeting the condition that the former expression is to stand for whatever it is about *A* which, unlike his merit, has *individual* worth.

We are also meeting another condition: that the equality of human worth be justification, or ground, of equal human rights. I can best bring this out by reverting to the visitor from Mars who had asked a little earlier why we want equalization of security benefits. Let us conjure up circumstances in which his question would spring, not from idle curiosity, but from a strong conviction that this, or any other, right entailing such undiscriminating equality of benefits, would be entirely *un*reasonable. Suppose then that he hails from a strict meritarian community, which maintains the *M*-system in its political life and analogous patterns in other associations. And to make things simpler, let us also suppose that he is shown nothing in New York or elsewhere that is out of line with our formal professions of equality, so that he imagines us purer, more strenuous, equalitarians than we happen to be. The pattern of valuation he ascribes to us then seems to him fantastically topsy-turvy. He can hardly bring himself to believe that rational human beings should want equal personal rights, legal and moral, for their "riff-raff" and their élites. Yet neither can he explain away our conduct as pure automatism, a mere fugue of social habit. "These people, or some of them," he will be saying to himself, "must have some reasons for this incredible code. What could these be?" If we volunteered an answer couched in terms of human worth, he might find it hard to understand us. Such an answer, unglossed, would convey to him no more than that we recognize something which is highly and equally valuable in all persons, but has nothing to do with their merit, and constitutes the ground of their equal rights. But this might start him hunting—snark-hunting—for some special quality named by "human worth" as honesty is named by "honesty" and kindness by "kindness," wondering all the while how it could have happened that he and all his tribe have had no inkling of it, if all of them have always had it.[42]

[42] Cf. Melden, *Rights and Right Conduct*, p. 80.

But now suppose that we avail ourselves of the aforesaid translation. We could then tell him: "To understand our code you should take into account how very different from yours is our own estimate of the relative worth of the welfare and freedom of different individuals. We agree with you that not all persons are capable of experiencing the same values. But there is a wide variety of cases in which persons are capable of this. Thus, to take a perfectly clear case, no matter how *A* and *B* might differ in taste and style of life, they would both crave relief from acute physical pain. In that case we would put the same value on giving this to either of them, regardless of the fact that *A* might be a talented, brilliantly successful person, *B* 'a mere nobody.' On this we would disagree sharply. You would weigh the welfare of members of the élite more highly than that of 'riff-raff,' as you call them. We would not. If *A* were a statesman, and giving him relief from pain enabled him to conclude an agreement that would benefit millions, while *B*, an unskilled laborer, was himself the sole beneficiary of the like relief, we would, of course, agree that the *instrumental* value of the two experiences would be vastly different—but not their *intrinsic* value. In all cases where human beings are capable of enjoying the same goods, we feel that the intrinsic value of their enjoyment is the same. In just this sense we hold that (1) *one man's well-being is as valuable as any other's.* And there is a parallel difference in our feeling for freedom. You value it only when exercised by good persons for good ends. We put no such strings on its value. We feel that choosing for oneself what one will do, believe, approve, say, see, read, worship, has its own intrinsic value, the same for all persons, and quite independently of the value of the things they happen to choose. Naturally, we hope that all of them will make the best possible use of their freedom of choice. But we value their exercise of that freedom, regardless of the outcome; and we value it equally for all. For us (2) *one man's freedom is as valuable as any other's.*"

This sort of explanation, I submit, would put him in a position to resolve his dilemma. For just suppose that, taking this homily at face-value, he came to think of us as believing (1) and (2).[43] No

---

[43] I am bypassing the factual question of the extent to which (1) and (2) are generally believed.

matter how unreasonable he might think of us he would feel it entirely reasonable that, since we do believe in equal *value* of human well-being and freedom, we should also believe in the *prima facie* equality of men's *right* to well-being and to freedom. He would see the former as a good reason for the latter; or, more formally, he could think of (1) and (2) respectively as the crucial premises in justification arguments whose respective conclusions would be: (3) One man's (*prima facie*) right to well-being is equal to that of any other, and (4) One man's (*prima facie*) right to freedom is equal to that of any other. Then, given (4), he could see how this would serve as the basis for a great variety of rights to specific kinds of freedom: freedom of movement, of association, of suffrage, of speech, of thought, of worship, of choice of employment, and the like. For each of these can be regarded as simply a specification of the general right to freedom, and would thus be covered by the justification of the latter. Moreover, given (3), he could see in it the basis for various welfare-rights, such as the right to education, medical care, work under decent conditions, relief in periods of unemployment, leisure, housing, etc.[44] Thus to give him (1) and (2) as justification for (3) and (4) would be to give him a basis for every one of the rights which are mentioned in the most complete of currently authoritative declarations of human rights, that passed by the Assembly of the United Nations in 1948. Hence to tell him that we believe in the equal worth of individual freedom and happiness would be to answer, in terms he can understand, his question, "What is your reason for your equalitarian code?"[45]

[44] I am well aware of the incompleteness of this highly schematic account. It does not pretend to give the full argument for the justification of (3) and (4) (and see next note) or of their "specifications." Among other omissions, it fails to make allowance for the fact that the complex inter-relations of these various rights would affect the justification of each.

[45] On p. 19 Frankena writes as though his own answer to the same question would be, "because 'all men are similarly capable of enjoying a good life' "; this, he says, is what "justifies the *prima facie* requirement that they be treated as equals." But that A and B are similarly capable of enjoying respectively good lives G(A) and G(B) is not a compelling reason for saying that A and B have equal right respectively to G(A) and G(B). The Brahmin who held (Sir Henry Maine, *Early History of Institutions* [New York, 1875], p. 399) that "a Brahmin was entitled to 20 times as much happiness as anyone else" need not have held that the Brahmin's *capacity* for happiness (or, for "enjoying a good life") differs in the

Nowhere in this defense of the translation of "equal human worth" into "equal worth of human well-being and freedom" have I claimed that the former can be *reduced* to the latter. I offered individual well-being and freedom simply as two things which do satisfy the conditions defined by individual human worth. Are there others? For the purposes of this essay this may be left an open question. For if there are, they would provide, at most, additional grounds for human rights. The ones I have specified are grounds enough. They are all I need for the analysis of equalitarian justice as, I trust, will appear directly.

III

I offer the following definition: An action is *just* if, and only if, it is prescribed exclusively by regard for the rights of all whom it affects substantially.[46] This definition could be discussed at length. I shall make, and with the utmost brevity, just two general points by way of elucidation:

(a) The standard cases are clearly covered, e.g., that of the judge adjudicating a dispute. To perform justly this strictly judicial func-

---

same ratio from that of others. All he would have to deny would be the equal *value* of the happiness of Brahmins and of others. It is some such premise as this that Frankena must affirm to bring off his justification-argument. I might add that I am not objecting to listing capacity among the premises. The only reason I did not is that I was only citing the "crucial" premise, the one that would be normally decisive for the acceptance or rejection of the justificandum. A reference to capacity would also be necessary, and I would follow Frankena in conceding that "men may well be different in such a way that the best life of which one is capable simply is not as good as that of which another is capable" (p. 20), adding a like concession in the case of freedom. *A*'s and *B*'s *prima facie* equal rights to well-being and to freedom are in effect equal rights to that well-being and freedom of which *A* and *B* are equally capable. Thus where the capacity for freedom is severely limited (e.g., that of an idiot or anyone else in the *non compos mentis* class), the right to freedom would be correspondingly limited.

[46] "Substantially" is deliberately and unavoidably vague (as much so as is the *"minimis"* in the legal maxim *de minimis non curat lex*). No general rule can be given that would apply to all the cases that would have to be considered. As to the definition as a whole, there is nothing original about it. It is adapted from Ulpian's *justitia est constans et perpetua voluntas jus suum cuique tribuendi, Dig.* 1, 1, 10, pr., which is in turn adapted from the oldest one on record (the "ancient formula" to which Frankena alludes), "justice consists in rendering to every man his due" (Plato, *Republic* 331, paraphrasing the poet Simonides).

tion[47] he must (i) seek to determine with scrupulous care what, in these circumstances, are the rights of the litigants and of others, if any, who are substantially affected,[48] and then (ii) render a verdict determined by regard for those rights and by nothing else. He may be unjust by failing at (i) through ignorance, carelessness, impatience, laziness, addiction to stereotypes of race or class, and the like; at (ii) by any sort of partiality, even if this is due to nothing so low as venality or prejudice, but perhaps even to humane and generous sentiments. Thus, if in the case before him an honest and upright man has trespassed on the rights of a well-known bully (perhaps only to protect one of the latter's victims), the judge will have no choice but to find for the bully: he must be "blind" to anything but the relevant rights when making up his verdict. This is the commonsense view of the matter, and it accords perfectly with what follows from the definition.

(b) The definition does not flout common usage by making "just" *interchangeable* with "right," and "unjust" with "wrong." Whenever the question of regard, or disregard, for substantially affected rights does not arise, the question of justice, or injustice, does not arise. We see a man wasting his property and talents in dissolute living. It would not occur to us to think of his conduct as unjust, unless we see it as having a substantial effect on somebody's rights, say, those of dependents: it is unfair or unjust *to* them.[49] Again, whenever one is in no position to govern one's action by regard for rights, the question of justice, or injustice, does not arise. Two strangers are in immediate danger of drowning off the dock on which I stand. I am the only one present, and the best I can do is to save one while the other drowns. Each has a right to my help, but I cannot give it to both. Hence regard for rights does not prescribe what I am to do, and neither "just" nor "unjust" will apply: I am not unjust to the one who drowns, nor just to the one I save.

[47] I am not here concerned with the judge's quasi-legislative function.

[48] E.g., the public.

[49] If we hold that every man has rights against himself, then there would be injustice to himself even if he had no dependents and no substantial obligations to others. Linguistic objections to this result would not affect the definition. If "injustice to himself" is strained, it is no more so than "rights against himself."

A major feature of my definition of "just" is that it makes the answer to "Is *x* just?" (where *x* is any action, decision, etc.) strictly dependent on the answer to another question: "What are the rights of those who are substantially affected by *x*?" [50] The definition cannot, and does not pretend that it can, give the slightest help in answering the latter question, with but one exception: it does tell us that the substantially affected rights, whatever they may be, should all be impartially respected. Thus it does disclose one right, though a purely *formal* one: the right to have one's *other* rights respected as impartially as those of any other interested party. But what are these other rights? Are they equal or unequal? On this the definition is silent. It is thus completely neutral in the controversy between meritarians and equalitarians, and should prove equally acceptable to either party.[51] Its neutralism should not be held against it. The words "just" and "unjust" are not the private property of the equalitarians; they may be used as conscientiously by those who reject, as by those who share, their special view of justice. We are not compelled to provide for this in our definitions; but there are obvious advantages in doing so. For we thereby offer our opponents common ground on which they too may stand while making their case. We allow Aristotle, for instance, to claim, without misusing language, that slavery and the disfranchisement of manual workers are just institutions. It allows us to rebut his claim, not by impugning its linguistic propriety, but by explaining that we affirm what his claim implicitly denies: that all human beings have the right to personal and political freedom.

It should now be plain to the reader why I have been so heavily preoccupied with the question of human rights throughout the first half of this essay, and content to write most of Section II without even mentioning the word "justice." I have done so precisely because my purpose in this essay is not to discuss justice in general, but equalitarian justice. As should now be obvious, had I tried to reason from the concept of justice to that of equalitarian justice I

[50] Cf. J. Pieper, *Justice,* trans. Lawrence Lynch (New York: Pantheon Books, 1955), pp. 13ff.
[51] Unless, of course, each is bent on putting his special view of justice into the definition of the word.

would have been reasoning in a circle. I did allude at the start to important historical and linguistic ties of justice with equality. But these, while perfectly relevant, are obviously not conclusive. They would be dismissed by a determined and clear-headed opponent, like Plato, as mere evidences of a widespread *mis*conception of justice. I am not suggesting that we should yield him this point or that, conversely, there is any good reason to think that he would come around to our view if we presented him with the argument of Section II (or a stronger one to the same effect). My contention is rather that we would be misrepresenting our view of justice if we were to give him the idea that it is susceptible of proof by that kind of historical and linguistic evidence. To explain our position to him so that, quite apart from his coming to agree with it, he would at least have the chance to *understand* it, one thing would matter above all: to show that we believe in human rights, and why.

That is why the weight of the argument in the preceding Section II fell so heavily on the notion of human worth, understood to mean nothing less than the equal worth of the happiness and freedom of all persons. Given this, we have equal welfare-rights and freedom-rights; and this puts us in a position to cover the full range of human rights which the natural rights tradition left so perplexingly indeterminate. I did not stop to argue for this contention when I made it in Section II, and will not do so now, for I have more important business ahead of me. I have not forgotten the task I set myself at the close of Section I, and wish to proceed to it as soon as possible. But before proceeding to this in Section IV, there is a major item of still unfinished business that must be attended to. It concerns a feature of equalitarian justice that must be made fully explicit, if only because it will play an important role in the argument that is to follow in Section IV.

Consider the following very simple rule of just distribution: *If A and B have sole and equal right to* x, *they have a joint right to the whole of* x. This rule (R_1) would be normally taken as axiomatic. Thus if *A* and *B* had sole and equal right to an estate, no executor bent on making a just settlement of their claims would think of giving away a part of the estate to some other person, *C*. But why not? Can it be shown that the consequent of R_1 does follow from its antecedent? It can. *Only* A *and* B *have any right to* x entails *anyone other than* A *or* B *has no right to* x and hence C *has no right to* x. Hence if some part of *x* were distributed to *C*, it would be going to someone who has no right to it. Such a distribution would not conform to our definition of "just": it would not be the one prescribed by impartial regard for the relevant rights. Now what if the executor withheld some part of *x* from *A* or *B,* without giving it to a third party? But how could that happen? Did he perhaps abandon it in a deserted place? He has no right to do that with any property unless it happens to be *his own.* So if he did such a foolish thing with a part of the estate, he has acted as though *he* is the third party to whom this has been distributed, and most unjustly, since he has no right to it. But what if he actually destroyed a part, perhaps throwing it overboard in a strong-box stuffed with valuables to sink to the bottom of the ocean? This too he would have no right to do, unless this part of the property were already *his.* So this action would be as unjust as before and for the same reason. And there is no other possibility, unless a part of the estate were lost, or destroyed through some natural calamity, in which case the question of its being *withheld* by the executor from *A* and *B* would not arise.[52] If he does withhold it, he would have to give it to some third party or else act as though he had already given it to himself, hence in either case to someone who has no right to *x,* hence unjustly. To act justly he must give the whole of it to those who have sole right to it.

Now let us think of an allied case. A man leaves a will containing many marks of his affection for his two sons and sole heirs and of his wish to benefit them. The terms of his will provide, *inter alia,* that a large industrial property is to be used, at the direction of trustees, to produce income for the sole and equal benefit of *D* and *E*, the income to be divided annually between them. Here the annual distribution of the income will fall directly under R_1. But another decision, in which *D* and *E* have as big a stake, will not: how the property is to be used to yield the desired income. Let *L*

---

[52] The only question then would be that of culpable negligence on the executor's part while the property was in his custody. And that is another matter.

and M be the only known feasible dispositions of the property for this purpose between which the trustees must decide at a given time: each, let us say, would involve a five-year commitment, but L would assure the estate twice the income, security, etc. being the same. L is obviously a windfall for the estate, and the trustees are not likely to waste a second thought on M as a possibly just decision in the circumstances. Why not? Why is it that in fairness to D and E they *should* choose L? Not in virtue of R_1, since that does not apply here: L is not a whole of which M is a part. What the trustees must be invoking (or would be, if they were thinking out the basis of their decision) is an analogue to R_1, covering cases such as this, where the right is not to an already existing object but to a future benefit which may be secured at any one of several possible levels: *if* D *and* E *have sole and equal right to benefit from* x, *they have a joint right to the benefit at the highest level at which it may be secured.* If we were asked to justify this rule (R_2), how would we go about it? If the trustees' reason for preferring M to L were to benefit a third party, C, the reasoning would be the same as before: since only D and E have the right to benefit from x, C has no such right; hence M cannot be the disposition prescribed by regard for the relevant rights. But what if the trustees were to prefer M, without aiming to benefit a third party? This possibility would be analogous to the case above in which R_1 was violated by the wilful loss or destruction of part of x. For a preference for M would be fully as injurious to D and E, and as unjust to them, as if the trustees had voted for L with the diabolical rider that half the annual income during the next five years was to be withheld from D and E and destroyed. The loss to D and E would be exactly the same, and the injustice would be the same: the trustees might have the right to forgo a benefit to *themselves* equivalent to the difference between L and M, but only if *they* had the right to this benefit in the first place. In choosing M over L they would be acting as though they did have this right, hence in clear violation of D's and E's *sole* right.

Now the validity of R_2 is obviously unaffected by the number of those who have sole and equal right to a benefit. It would hold for any number; hence for the whole of humanity, or any lesser part of it. Consider then the total benefit derivable by humanity from men's use of what we may call "the means of well-being," i.e., of their own bodies and minds and of the resources of the natural universe. Since men have an equal right to well-being[53] (apart from special property-rights, and the like, with which we are not now concerned), they have an equal right to the means of well-being. And the right of humanity to these means is exclusive.[54] We are, therefore, entitled to assert that *men have sole and equal right to benefit from the means of well-being.* From this we may conclude, in conformity with R_2, that *men are jointly entitled to this benefit at the highest level at which it may be secured.*

This conclusion affects importantly the concept of equalitarian justice. It implies that the fundamental and distinctive idea in its notion of just distribution is (i) not equal distribution of benefits, but (ii) their equal distribution at the highest obtainable level. (i) has already been argued for in Frankena's essay when he considered, and rejected, Hourani's attractive formula, "Justice is equality, evident or disguised," as an over-simplification. But on Frankena's view neither can (ii) constitute the needed corrective. It is an obligation of beneficence, not of justice, he argues, "to promote the greatest possible good." He writes: "even if we allow . . . that society has an obligation to be beneficent, then we must insist that such beneficence, at least if it exceeds a certain minimum, is no part of social justice as such." [55] Now there is no difference of opinion between us as to the importance of distinguishing sharply the concept of beneficence (or of benevolence) from that of equalitarian justice. But I submit that this can be done perfectly by adhering to the concept of equalitarian justice I have given here, and is in no way imperilled by my thesis here at (ii). To go back to the definition of "just" at the start: this leaves plenty of scope for acts which might be beneficent but *un*just, as, e.g., when A defrauds B to help C; or

[53] Proposition (3) near the close of Section II.
[54] Or, at any rate, it may be so regarded for the purposes of this argument. To take account of the rights of other animals, we would only need to add "except for the rights of other animals" before the italicized portion of the premise and the conclusion of the ensuing argument, and the validity of the inference would be unaffected.
[55] *Supra,* p. 6.

beneficent and *non*-just (neither just nor unjust: "just" does not apply), as when *A* helps one needy person, disregarding the claim of millions of others for the simple reason that he is in no position to help more than one out of all these millions. Conversely, neither would it follow from my theory of equalitarian justice that every just act, decision, practice, etc., will be beneficent. A large number will be non-beneficent (neither beneficent nor maleficent; "beneficent" will not apply): the repayment of debts, the rendering of ordinary judicial verdicts, or the enforcement of punishments. So *equalitarian justice* and *beneficence* will have different extensions, and their meanings will be as different as is that of *justice* on the present definition from that of *beneficence* on the usual view. Hence the concepts are entirely distinct, both intensionally and extensionally. But distinct concepts may, of course, overlap. And this is precisely what I maintain in the present case: (ii) above certainly falls under beneficence; but that, of itself, is no reason whatever why it *may* not *also* fall under equalitarian justice. That it does is what the foregoing argument for the validity of R_2, and its applicability to human rights, was designed to show.

One way of stating the thesis of that argument would be that equalitarian justice has a direct stake not only in equalizing the distribution of those goods whose enjoyment constitutes well-being, but also in promoting their creation. That it would have an indirect stake in the latter even if it were concerned *only* with equalizing their distribution could be argued independently by an obvious generalization of the point I made at the start of Section II, where I argued that a more affluent society could "buy more equality." The reasoning for and from R_2 provides a stronger and more general argument that *given any two levels of the production of good known to be possible in given circumstances, then,* other things being equal, *the higher should be preferred on grounds of justice.* "Goods" here, as throughout this essay, is a general expression for a class of which economic goods would be a sub-class. We may thus use an economic test-case of the underlined proposition: Suppose that the supreme policy-maker of the *N*'s (whose economy resembles closely that of the U.S.A.) had to choose between two policies, P(*L*) and P(*M*), knowing that (a) the effect of P(*M*) would be to maintain throughout the next five years the current rate of annual increase of the gross national product (which is, say, 2.5 per cent), while that of P(L) would *double* that rate; (b) the pattern of distribution of the national income would remain the same; (c) the greater wealth produced under P(L) would not be offset by aggravation of the risk of war, cultural deterioration, corruption of morals, or of any other significant evil.[56] (c) is, of course, a strong restriction; but, like (b), it is built into the hypothesis to insure that the *only* appreciable difference between the two policies would be in the lesser, or fuller, utilization and expansion of the economic resources of the nation. This, and the artificiality of the whole model, by no means trivializes the contention that in such circumstances equalitarian justice would leave the policy-maker no choice but P(L). To say that beneficence (or benevolence) would leave him no other choice *would* be trivial: no one would care to dispute this. But the same thing said for equalitarian justice can be, and is being, disputed. This asserts that the N's have *rights* in this matter which the policy maker would violate if he were to choose P(M)—as much so as the trustees in the example would violate the rights of D and E if they chose M. That the rights of the N's, unlike those of D and E, are moral, not legal, is immaterial: *only* the moral justice of the decision is here in view. The moral rights in question are those of the N's to well-being, hence to the means of well-being: to anything which would enrich their life, save it from pain, disease, drudgery, emptiness, ugliness. Given (a) in the hypothesis, an enormously larger quantity of such means would be made available to the N's under P(L) in the course of the five-year period; and given (b) their distribution would be no more unequal than that of the smaller volume of goods produced under P(M). Hence the N's have jointly a right to P(L). They have this for just the reasons which justify the inference from the antecedent of R_2 to its consequent. The crux of the inference is that since the N's, and only they, have a right to the benefits obtainable under either alternative, they have a right to that alternative which produces the

---

[56] Perhaps we should add (d), that P (L) would have no adverse effect on the economy of other nations and would not decrease the disposition of the N's to help needier nations.

greater benefit. Only (and at most) if the policy-maker had *himself* the right to the aggregate benefit represented by the difference between $P(L)$ and $P(M)$ would he have the right to frustrate the realization of that benefit. But he does not have that right. So if he were to choose $P(M)$ he would violate the right of those who do. That is why that decision would be unjust.

Two more points:

(A) That not equality as such, but equality at the highest possible level, is the requirement of equalitarian justice may be argued as strongly in the case of the right to freedom.[57] Thus if a legislature had before it two bills, $B(L)$ and $B(M)$, such that $B(L)$ would provide for greater personal freedom than would $B(M)$, then, other things remaining equal, they would be voting unjustly if they voted for the second: they would be violating the human right to freedom of those affected by the legislation. A vote for $B(M)$ would be tantamount to a vote for the needless[58] *restriction* of freedom. And since *freedom* is a personal (or individual) right, to equalize its restriction would be to aggravate, not to alleviate, its injustice. Would any of us feel that no injustice was suffered by Soviet citizens by the suppression of *Doctor Zhivago* if we were reliably informed that no one, not even Khrushchev, was exempted, and that the censors themselves had been foreign mercenaries?

(B) The conjunction of equalitarian justice and benevolence could have been argued at a still deeper level if we had gone down to the ultimate *reasons* for the equal right to well-being and freedom, i.e., to (1) and (2) at the close of Section II above. What could be a stronger expression of benevolence towards one's fellow-men, than to say that the well-being and freedom of every one of them is worth as much as one's own and that of those few persons one happens to love? At this level equalitarian justice is as deeply committed to two notions which it does not display in its title, benevolence and freedom, as to the notion of equality, which it does. It now remains

---

[57] Cf. the first principle of justice in J. B. Rawls, "Justice as Fairness," *Philosophical Review* 67 (1958), pp. 164ff., at p. 165; reprinted in F. Olafson, *Justice and Social Policy* (Englewood Cliffs, N. J.: Prentice-Hall, 1961).

[58] Since we are stipulating that other things would be equal.

to show how, given this threefold commitment, it can *also* recognize claims of *un*equal distribution.

IV

Why is it just to distribute good according to merit? I shall answer this for one distributable good which I shall call "praise," using this word to cover all direct expressions of admiration, appreciation, or approval of merit which are subject to voluntary control. This is an extended use of the word, but it has definite limits. Thus if *A* and *B* are competing for an office, the mere fact of *C*'s appointing *A* is not to count as praise from *C* to *A*, no matter how emphatic be the approval of *A*'s merit it is understood to imply. To qualify as praise something more direct or express would be needed, though not necessarily in verbal form. Thus *C* would not have to congratulate *A* on the appointment, or tell him he has the good qualities the job calls for; it would be enough to convey as much to him by one's demeanor or facial expression.

A man should not be praised for merit he does not have. Indiscriminate praise is a fake; and to fake praise in special cases is to cheapen it, and hence to violate the equal right of all persons to be praised in a sound currency, if they are to be praised at all. It does not follow from this, nor is it true, that merit has to be the necessary *and* sufficient condition of giving praise. At times we would not praise a person unless we felt he needed a special reassurance or encouragement. But far more frequently merit *is* sufficient. Take our ordinary response to a delightful conversationalist, for example. In the various subtle, but unmistakable, ways in which we manifest our approval we measure out to him sizeable quantities of what some economists, without intending to be humorous, call "psychic income." We know that to give this is to please him. But the question of his need of it is not a factor in our giving it, any more than the landlord's need is a factor in the tenant's payment of the rent. And this is what happens in the majority of cases. This is "the generally expected thing" when praise is given in our society, and this is what I shall call the practice of *praising for merit ("mp")* or *giving praise according to merit.* If we did not have *mp,* it would be understood that no person, or only some privileged persons (e.g., the monarch, the nobility, Aryans, members of the Communist Party, Platonic philosophers), have the right to praise any person they choose on the sole ground of his merit.

Mp is a "practice" in the somewhat technical sense this term has acquired in recent moral philosophy.[59] For my present purpose two important points are involved here: (a) *mp* may be formulated in terms of a set of rules, conformity to which depends on voluntary compliance with (or, obedience to) the rules. Thus one of the rules would be, "Those in a position to praise both *A* and *B* should give more praise to *A* if his merit is the greater." One's compliance with this rule is not forced by the *fact* that *A* has the greater merit, nor by one's *belief* that he has. *C* might be well aware of the fact, yet lavish praise on *B*, cold-shouldering *A* (perhaps because he is fond of *B* and hates *A*). That the rule can be disobeyed in this and other ways proves that the usual compliance with it is voluntary. (b) In the absence of *mp*, actions which are now understood as praising for merit would be normally understood very differently even if they had, in all other respects, the same characteristics.[60] Thus suppose that *mp* did not exist, while praising for need did. In such a society the conduct by *C* just described would be construed very differently. No one would take it as an unfavorable reflection on *A*'s merit, and *A* could not feel slighted by it; from *C*'s excessive praise for *B*, *A* would merely gather that *C* has an exaggerated idea of *B*'s need of encouragement. *Not* to be praised in that society would be itself a kind of tribute.

If this is what *mp* means, then the distribution of praise under this practice is bound to reflect to some degree inequalities in the distribution of merit. To live with *mp* is to live in a world in which some people will get this kind of "psychic income" in abundance, while others must subsist on miserable pittances of it.[61] For this

[59] See especially J. B. Rawls, "Two Concepts of Rules," *Philosophical Review* 64 (1955), pp. 3ff.; reprinted in F. Olafson, *Society, Law, and Morality* (Englewood Cliffs, N. J.: Prentice-Hall, 1961).

[60] Cf. Rawls, *op. cit.*, p. 25.

[61] In any society that puts a high premium on individual achievement something like this will always be true, so far as I can see, even after taking full account of mitigating factors, such as (a) that the varieties of merit are legion, so that

reason equalitarian justice would have no choice but to condemn *mp* as an inherently unjust practice, *if* equality in the distribution of good were its only concern. But from the account of it in Section III we know that it is also concerned that happiness and freedom be secured at the highest possible levels. Let us see what difference this makes.

But first let us take account of a matter of fact: that the effect of praising an achievement is generally to enhance the relevant creative effort. To say this is not to deny that sometimes praise has no effect and sometimes a bad effect. But if it were *generally* ineffective the argument I am about to make for it would fail. And *every* argument for it would fail if its normal effect were sufficiently bad—if, say, it were like that of alcohol on alcoholics. If it demoralized all, or most, people, praise would be as vile as flattery, or viler; only a few poisonous individuals would indulge in it. The actual facts are reassuringly different, in spite of occasional swelled heads. What happens for the most part is that in praising a meritorious performance we give its merit our backing. We thereby help the performer, giving him the incentive to attain again the same merit, or a higher one. We even help ourselves: by going on record in favor of the meritorious performance we are more likely to emulate it ourselves in the future. This being the case, the proponent of equalitarian justice cannot judge *mp* fairly unless he connects it with his interest in getting all human beings to be as creative as possible, i.e., to bring into existence, to the best of their ability, those values which will enrich their own life and that of others. This gives him at once a strong initial interest in *mp* as a practice generating incentives to creative effort. And since *mp* can exist *alongside* of other incentive-generating practices (and always has in every known society), its presence in a given society represents a net addition (and a substantial one) to the aggregate stimuli to creative effort. A society with *mp*, therefore, would have a higher level of production of good than it would have without *mp*. But as has been argued in Section III,

---

some who fail at one kind of performance may shine at another, and (b) that praise may rightly be given not for absolute achievement but for achievement in some proportion to ability, so that a tiny success may rate high praise at times.

given any two levels of production of good known to be possible in given circumstances, then, other things being equal, the higher should be preferred on grounds of justice.

This would provide a utilitarian argument for the justice of *mp* (justifying it as a means to an end which justice approves), *if* the "other things being equal" clause can be made good.

To make up our minds on this "if," let us first be clear about the fact that *mp* as such does not require, or even favor, inequality in the distribution of any of the *other* goods (goods other than praise) whose creation it tends to enhance. How equally or unequally these are going to be distributed will depend on decisions which are entirely distinct from the decision to maintain *mp*. Thus it would be sheer confusion to think that there would be any incompatibility between deciding to distribute praise according to merit and economic goods according to need. The most starry-eyed equalitarian, intent on running his whole economy on the latter maxim, could afford to be as much of an enthusiast for *mp* as anyone else; indeed he would have good reason to be much more of one: having denied himself the usual economic incentives, he would have to work this one for all it was worth. As this example may suggest, *mp* fits a generally equalitarian society not only as well as a meritarian one, but better. But I do not wish to make anything of this last point. All that is needed for the present argument is that the practice of *mp* as such cannot be held *generally* responsible for inequalities in the distribution of goods in the society, but only for those inherent in its own operation, i.e., inequalities in the distribution of praise itself. The question then is whether *these* inequalities will be so repugnant to justice as to constitute offsetting factors against the tonic effect of *mp* on human productivity which our concept of justice approves. When we narrow down the question in this way I think it can be shown that they will not be repugnant to justice at all, and will not only leave "other things equal," but better than equal.

To simplify the problem to the utmost let us think of a purely economic society of two individuals, *A* and *B*, *A* being the more efficient producer. An angel is set over them, whose good will for each of them is boundless. If he could measure out to them well-being directly from some celestial storehouse, he would be giving vast and equal measures to each. Such direct munificence is unfortunately denied him. He has been told that whatever well-being is to come to A and B must reach them entirely through their own efforts; all the angel can do for them is to propose to them new practices. He now puts his mind on whether or not he should offer them mp, which they have hitherto done without. To isolate the probable effect of mp itself on their lives, he pegs the solution on two assumptions: (a) that they will operate it fairly (for if they did not, the results would not be an indication of the use of mp, but of its misuse); (b) the expected increment in their joint product is to be divided in the same ratio as at present (for there is nothing about mp to require any special ratio, hence any ratio different from the present). He then sees that, on these conditions, A and B have both much to gain from the new arrangement: the economic income of each will increase; and each will get some of the newly created "psychic income," though A, the more meritorious producer, will get more of this than B.[62] If these were the only results of the change, the angel would have no reason to hesitate between leaving them in their present state or giving them mp. He would give it to them, and not because of having any preference, even the slightest, for the well-being of A over that of B, but precisely because he has the same desire to increase the happiness of both as much as possible in the circumstances of his choice, i.e., circumstances in which he must choose either for the *status quo* or for their present way of life as modified by mp.[63]

But, of course, there may be another result from the change: the mere fact that A will be made happier than B (A can count on getting the larger share of the praise) may make B unhappy, and so much so that his unhappiness from just this source might be

[62] The reader should not be offended by the psychological crudity of this and ensuing remarks. I am trying to get this model to answer just one kind of question.

[63] The reader may want to know why the angel is limiting his decision-problem in just this way and is giving no consideration to other alternatives to the *status quo*. The answer has already been given in my earlier remark that mp can exist alongside of other incentive-generating practices; therefore the question of introducing it need not be complicated by giving it a comparative rating against such practices; A and B may have a variety of other practices and mp as well.

great enough to outbalance his gains and even (if we allow the angel some way of determining such things) A's gains as well. This possibility could be quite enough to disrupt totally the angel's calculations. Whether or not mp will prove a blessing or a curse will now turn on how B takes it; and B knowing this could use it to blackmail the angel against even making the offer: B need only announce that he would make himself miserable enough to offset the expected gains. Fortunately the situation has a saving feature: A and B are moral beings. This has not been stated; but it is certainly implied in assumption (a), for only moral beings could operate this practice fairly. Our angel then can ask B to look at mp as a moral being should, hence with equal regard for A's well-being as for his own. If he did so, B would not be made unhappy merely because A became happier than himself, that is to say, out of envy. To say this to B is not, alas, to assure him that he will react to the effects of the practice as a moral being should, thereby saving himself the misery of jealousy. No one can insure this for B except (at most) B himself and by his own effort. All the angel can tell B is that he should make this effort; but that, in any case, B cannot bring up any unfavorable results due to *envy* as a reason against the *justice* of the proposed institution. To allow such reasons to count would ruin the prospects of giving a moral justification of any practice: by the same token unhappiness due to arrogance (i.e., to the demand for special privilege) would also count, and that would be the end of justice.

The upshot of the argument is simply this: *because* (not in spite) of his equal concern for the happiness of all persons, a proponent of equalitarian justice would have good reason to approve *mp, given* its stimulating effect on the creation of those goods whose enjoyment constitutes happiness, *unless* the effect were offset by others repugnant to his sense of justice. But there are no such effects. The fact that envious people are made unhappy by an institution is no evidence of its injustice.

This is not the only argument for *mp*, or even the strongest. There are two others which deserve at least as full a treatment, but fortunately do not require it. I shall make them in the most summary fashion to compensate for the unavoidable length of the one

I have just finished. Both of them argue from the right to freedom.

(1) Praising for merit is something people like to do, and do spontaneously when they are left free to talk and laugh and applaud without restraints from political or clerical or domestic martinets. It is thus a direct expression of human freedom, and such a pervasive one that it spreads over every area of life, private or public. To try to suppress this practice would involve enormous inroads on personal liberty.

(2) Over and above its coincidence, for the reason just given, with one of the major *ends* of freedom (that of expressing without impediment one's actual feelings about one's fellows' character and conduct), it is also an indispensable *means* for another such end: that of diffusing widely among the population free choices between competing values. It is like "consumer's vote" in a free economy: it gives the consumers of the values produced in a society a means of influencing the producers, and thus a share in determining which values are produced and in what proportions. Its obvious disadvantage is its lack of any facilities for aggregating and recording the results of individual decisions, either directly, as through elections, or indirectly, as through the market. But it has the advantage of being as equally distributed as the suffrage, while extending, and more flexibly, to even larger and more varied sets of choices than those of the market.

With this case for the justice of the practice of praising for merit thus laid out before us, let us take stock of what has been accomplished and how. I have taken the maxim, "to each according to his merit," as in need of justification, and have undertaken to derive it from a set of propositions which includes only equalitarian value-premises (those from which the equal right of human beings to well-being and freedom is derived) plus one or more factual premises. Since I limited the demonstration to the special proposition, "to each *praise* according to his merit," I needed such factual premises as that the general effect of so distributing praise enhances the production of value and offers a useful device for its control by the free responses of private individuals. From each of these we get an instrumental, or utilitarian, justification: we justify this way of distributing praise because it is a means to the advancement of those ends which are stated in our value-premises, such as the well-being and the freedom to which all persons have a severally equal and jointly exclusive right. We also get a collateral non-instrumental justification in terms of freedom: praising for merit is itself one of the forms in which persons choose to express their freedom. Since merit is unequal, to justify mp is to justify unequal rights in respect of praise. The whole argument then falls into the following form: Because persons have *equal* rights to well-being and to freedom, then, in the special circumstances of distributing praise for merit (those noticed in the factual premises of the argument) their right to this particular good is *un*equal. If we then think of the latter as an exception, or as a whole class of exceptions, to men's equal right to enjoyable good, we are in a position to justify the exception in the way in which I said earlier (at the close of Section I) exceptions to natural rights should be justified. The moral (as distinct from the factual) reasons given for this exception to the equal right to good have been only such reasons as were built into our concept of equalitarian justice and would be given as the reasons for all our natural rights: men's joint and equal right to well-being and freedom at the highest obtainable level.

But apart from the theoretical import of this argument, it has useful practical implications. In telling us why we *may* justly distribute praise unequally according to merit, it tells us also what we may *not* do. In general it warns us against confusing merit with human worth, and against allowing merit to swamp human worth. It reminds us that terms like "superior" and "inferior," properly applicable to a person's merit, are inapplicable to the person: there can be strictly and literally superior or inferior poets, teachers, bankers, garage-mechanics, actresses, statesmen; but there can be strictly and literally no superior or inferior persons, individuals, men. From this it follows that when we praise a man we must not praise him *as* a man. His humanity is not a fit subject for praise. To think otherwise is to incur a "category mistake," and one fraught with grave moral consequences. For given men's sensitiveness to honor and dishonor, when merit is made the measure of their human dignity, their own sense of dignity tends to become distorted. If they are talented and successful, praise misdirected from their achievements to their person will foster the illusion that they are superior persons, belong to a higher moral caste, and may claim on moral grounds a privileged status for their own well-being and freedom.[64] Conversely, if low achievement scores are not kept wholly distinct from personal worth, which does not register on any score, men may be made to feel that they are the human inferiors of others, that their own happiness or freedom has inferior worth. This would be a grave injustice. Any practice which tends to so weaken and confuse the personal self esteem of a group of persons—slavery, serfdom or, in our own time, racial segregation—may be morally condemned on this one ground, even if there were no other for indicting it. Some such ground is alluded to in the Court opinion in the decision which finally struck down segregation in the public schools.[65] That verdict could be reached more directly and extended to every form of racial segregation,[66] by applying the ideas that have been sketched in this essay. If one thinks of human worth as the moral foundation of all rights, one will see that the equal honor of persons is presupposed by the unequal honor that may be given to unequal merit and, hence, that no practice which habitually humiliates persons can be defended by differences of merit, real or imagined.

[64] The best example of this among philosophical moralists is Nietzsche: "Egoism belongs to the nature of a distinguished soul. I mean that immovable faith that other beings are by nature subordinate to a being such as 'we are'; that they should sacrifice themselves to us," *Beyond Good and Evil,* trans. Marianne Cowan (Chicago, 1935), p. 265. A little earlier (p. 258) he had praised that "good and healthy aristocracy" which "accepts with a clear conscience the sacrifice of an enormous number of men who must *for its sake* [that of the aristocracy] be suppressed and reduced to incomplete human beings, to slaves, to tools" (Nietzsche's italics).

[65] *Brown v. Topeka Board of Education,* 347 U.S. (1954), pp. 483ff., "To separate them from others of similar age and qualifications solely because of their race generates a feeling of inferiority as to their status in the community that may affect their hearts and minds in a way unlikely ever to be undone."

[66] The context in which the above citation is imbedded leaves one uncertain as to whether, in the opinion of the Court, (a) this evil was *per se* a reason for outlawing segregation in public schools, or (b) constituted such a reason merely because the "feeling of inferiority" reduced the children's chances of getting equal benefit from their schooling and thus disturbed the equality of their educational opportunities. The ensuing citation from the earlier finding in the Kansas case makes it look as though (b) expressed the Court's opinion; and (b) unlike (a), is not immediately generalizable to other forms of segregation.

Along similar lines I believe it may be argued that other differentials—in particular those of economic reward, economic power, and political power—can be justified on the terms of equalitarian justice. Given certain propositions which, if true, are true on empirical grounds, recording observable uniformities of human nature and conduct with which every moral philosophy must reckon, good *moral* reasons may be offered for inequalities of various kinds, which would be "just-making" reasons, the very same as those which would be offered for equalizing benefits of other kinds. And the very procedure which led to these results would contain built-in protections of human equality, limiting the differentials in income and in power by the very machinery which certifies their justice within the permissible range. To accomplish this would be to answer Plato's question, the one that started us off on this whole inquiry early in Section One. It would be to show him over what special form the three maxims of unequal distribution, "to each according to his merit, his work, and the agreements he has made," may be joined without theoretical inconsistency or moral compromise to the two maxims of equal distribution, "to each according to his need, and to his [human] worth."

Social Justice in
Social Dynamics

I propose to approach the problem of social justice as an economist and social scientist in a manner somewhat different from
that which is customary among the philosophers. The philosopher
treats the concept of justice as essentially a normative concept. He
is concerned with abstract notions of what is right, good, and just.
He is concerned with what ought to be, not necessarily with what
is. These normative discussions are important and I would not for a
moment wish to decry their value. There is, however, another point
of view from which the problem of social justice can be examined.
This might be called the *positive* or *operational* point of view in
which social justice—or at least the image of social justice as it
exists in the minds of the members of society—is an essential
variable in determining the dynamic processes and the evolution of
that society.

By "social dynamics," I mean neither more nor less than social
evolution; that is, the whole great process by which a society moves
from Monday to Tuesday to Wednesday and so on. Social evolution
is, of course, a process of extreme complexity. It can be illuminated,
however, by theoretical models which are drawn essentially from
the processes of biological evolution. Although there are great differences between biological evolution and social evolution, there
are important similarities as well. The most important point of

similarity is the fact that the notion of ecological succession and of a dynamic based on mutation and selection applies to both. Biological evolution can be regarded as a succession of short-run biological equilibria of the ecosystem. A pond, for instance, can be regarded as an equilibrium system of interacting populations of different chemical and biological species. This equilibrium is likely to survive small disturbances. If, for instance, ten per cent of one kind of fish are taken out of a pond, the proportions among the populations of the different species in the pond will be upset, but it is likely that in a year or two they will be re-established. Yet even in the absence of external forces, the equilibrium will gradually change over the long run because of certain irreversible factors in the very processes by which the equilibrium is maintained. The metabolic processes of life, for instance, absorb carbon from the air and the pond gradually will fill up and become a swamp. Mutations occur in the genetic materials of the different organic species. Most of these disturb the equilibrium for a while and disappear. Occasionally, however, one appears which gives the organism—and eventually the species—an advantage so great that a *new* and lasting population equilibrium takes the place of the old. Sometimes the ecological revolution is swift and dramatic: a small change in the environment produces a drastic change in the population of species. The precarious equilibrium of the forest and the prairie in the Middle West before the advent of civilization was an interesting example of this point.

Society, likewise, may be thought of as a large pond filled with interacting populations. In addition to biological and inorganic species, there are social species such as automobiles, schools, gas stations, teachers, clubs, philosophers, corporations, states, missiles, and ideas. It is the last of these which constitutes the essential difference between a social system and a biological system and between social evolution and biological evolution. Below the level of the human species, ideas or images are present only in a very rudimentary form: there are instincts that are genetically determined and behavior patterns which may properly be attributed to images— that is, to cognitive structures within the organisms concerned. These images, however, are not learned from experience, but are built into the organism by the growth process which is guided by the genes. The bird builds its nest and the spider spins its web because in some sense it "knows" how to do this, but this knowledge has not been created by a learning process and has not been erected by experience. The image, the instinct, is built into the organism itself by its genetic processes of growth.

The principle of learning from experience begins to appear in the evolutionary process only with the higher animals. A cat, for instance, behaves like a cat not only because of its genetic constitution but also because it has learned things from its mother as a kitten. In a very real sense, cats have a culture in a way that insects do not. In the development of the human species, however, still another principle comes onto the evolutionary stage. The human nervous system is capable of creating symbolic images and modifying and transmitting these images through speech. Cats teach through signs; humans teach through symbols. This seemingly small change has resulted in an enormous acceleration of the pace of evolution. Under the impact of man, the face of the earth and the composition of its species changes at a pace a hundred or even a thousand times greater than it had done previously. This pace accelerates all the time as social evolution produces more and more complex social forms.

One may be tempted to ask, "But what does this have to do with social justice?" The answer is that the images that men have of themselves and of the society around them—because of their impact on human behavior—are an important, indeed, almost a dominant element in the course of social evolution. In these images the idea of social justice plays a significant role. In an earlier work,[1] I developed a theory of human behavior (or at least a way of looking at it) as consisting essentially of setting in motion a course of events which is intended to carry the person into the most highly valued of his images of potential futures. This is, of course, an economist's way of looking at the matter: to regard behavior as being fundamentally subject to choice. Choice is a process by which we scan a number of possible futures and allot some ordinal numbers such as first, second, third, etc., to elements of this set, and

[1] *The Image* (University of Michigan Press, 1956).

pick out the element which is labeled first. All that is strictly necessary for this process is that we divide the set of possible futures into two sub-sets, one of which we label first and the other second. If the set labeled first contains only one element, this constitutes the chosen future and we behave accordingly.

The future, of course, does not always turn out as we expect, for the choice of a future does not necessarily guarantee it. The future, however, is determined by the choices that we make. That is, there will exist a set function relating the chosen future to the actual future. Thus suppose that $F_1, F_2, \ldots F_n$ is the set of images of the possible future, and $G_1, G_2, \ldots G_n$ is the set of actual futures. The choice of, say, F_1, does not necessarily mean that we shall proceed into the identically corresponding actual future G_1; it does mean, however, that for any F_1 that we select, there is some G_j which corresponds to it. For many choices, there is a high probability that G_j will, in fact, be the same as G_1, but this is not necessarily true.

If, for instance, I find myself lecturing at Swarthmore on March 19 of a certain year, it is because at some earlier time I had an image of time and space in which, out of all possible futures, my lecturing in Swarthmore on March 19 was labeled first in my value system. Because of this value preference, the formation of which is irrelevant here, I performed certain acts—such as telephoning a travel agency, picking up a plane ticket, driving to an airport, getting on a plane, and so on—all of which were designed in my image of cause and effect to make the image of the future correspond with the actuality. Without having formed and selected the image "in Swarthmore on March the 19th," I would certainly not be there. But the mere fact of my having the image, and of setting in motion certain behavior to realize it, did not guarantee that the image and the actual future would correspond. As I write this on March the 9th I must recognize a certain possibility that I will not be at Swarthmore on March the 19th. I may be taken ill; trains and planes may be immobilized by strikes, or Swarthmore may be hit by a nuclear bomb before that date. In the absence of extraordinary events, however, I shall be somewhat surprised if the actual future does not correspond to my image.

How does the image of social justice fit into this pattern of human behavior? My visit to Swarthmore is clearly—in my own eyes —good, or I would not go. I am not sure, however, that I have thought of this particular activity as being just or unjust either socially or individually. I might feel, I suppose, that it is unjust that I should be asked to give this lecture when Professor X obviously would have given a much better one. On the other hand, Professor X may have already been asked and refused, in which case the injustice is lessened. It may even be that the organizers of this lecture believed that, in fact, I am the best person to give it. In this they may be unwise and mistaken, but error, or lack of wisdom, does not constitute injustice. It may be also that the reward which I will get for the lecture, both the honorarium and the pleasure I will receive at being among old friends at Swarthmore, is more than I deserve. On the other hand, I am not sure that I can provide an operational definition of the concept of desert. If we all get our deserts, as Hamlet said, "Who should 'scape whipping?"

It may be that my total reward for giving this lecture is larger than the smallest amount for which I would have consented to come. In this case, I am getting what the economist calls *economic rent* or *economic surplus,* and this is perhaps in some sense unjust. If it is unjust, I must confess, it is a burden that I will bear with some equanimity. It is clear from this that my concept of social justice played a very small part in making the decision to come and give a lecture about it. This fact demonstrates that the image of social justice is not a universal element in that valuation process by which men come to decisions. There are, however, some choices in which the image of social justice plays an important part, and it is these which we must identify if we are to examine the role which the image of social justice plays in the dynamics of society.

Before proceeding in full cry after these decisions in which the image of social justice is significant or even dominant, let me pause for a moment to look at the role which is played in decision-making by the perception of divergences between a perceived real situation and a perceived ideal situation. The concept of perceived divergence between real and ideal values also plays a dominant role in the explanation of the behavior of what have come to be called *cybernetic* systems, or control systems. A thermostatic system, for instance, has an ideal temperature at which it is set, say 70°. It has a thermometer which enables it to "perceive" the actual temperature. If the actual temperature falls below the ideal, the system sets in motion behavior to warm things up. If the perceived actual temperature rises above the ideal, the system sets in action behavior which will result in cooling things down. This is the principle of homeostasis which is of such great importance in understanding what Cannon called the "wisdom of the body." This principle can also be invoked to explain a great deal of human behavior at the cognitive or affective level. We keep our friendships in repair by much the same process by which we keep a constant temperature in our bodies or in the house: if a friendship is cooling below our ideal level, a letter, a telephone call, or a Christmas card may warm it up. If a friend is getting a little too affectionate and demanding, there are many ways of increasing the social distance which will cool him down.

The wisdom of the spirit, of course, consists in knowing where to set the ideal. A purely homeostatic mechanism is—within wide limitations—quite indifferent as to where the ideal is set. My home thermostat will maintain a steady temperature anywhere between fifty and eighty degrees. It is up to me to set it at the level which best reconciles the claims of health, vitality, and comfort. As we move toward social systems, the problem of where to set the ideal becomes of increasing importance. There is what may be called a homeostatic apparatus within the social system, which acts to reduce divergences between perceived actual and ideal values. In this homeostatic sense, social justice is an ideal; that is, it is something divergence from which is perceived and acts as a cue to behavior.

The perception of divergence between the perceived real value and the ideal value of any important psychological variable—that is, of any variable which is strongly related to utility or general satisfaction—may be labeled *discontent*. In this sense, discontent can be regarded as the prime mover of man to action provided that his image of cause and effect permits him to believe himself capable of such action as to reduce the divergence between the perceived real and the ideal. We may notice a point here, the importance of which will be clearer later. The divergence between the real and the ideal may be reduced by acting so as to manipulate the real. But it may also be reduced by adjusting the ideal. This is the way of renunciation—of wanting what you get, rather than getting what you want. It is traditionally associated with Eastern philosophies, and if adopted it is a powerful deterrent to rapid change.

The adjustment of the ideal is not, of course, necessarily "irrational." If activity results in a continued failure to reduce the gap between the perceived real and the ideal, a person may follow one of three courses. He may change his perception. This may be dangerous if the perception differs much from something which we can call reality, but, on the other hand, it is also comforting. A man may say that his wife really loves him in spite of that fact that she continually hits him over the head with the frying pan. Modern studies of perception indicate that what we think of as sense data are, in fact, so strongly guided by existing beliefs and by our value system that we cannot afford to dismiss as immediately invalid the alteration of perception in response to homeostatic failure. Only one cheer, however, for this solution; we do well to be suspicious of it and to give at least two cheers for the second alternative, which is the readjustment of the ideal. At its worst, this can be a retreat into apathy or into criminality. But somewhere along the line, as the bloom of youth is knocked off us by our contact with the world, we make this kind of adjustment. The third reaction, and the only one for which I am inclined to give three cheers, is that of finding a new course of behavior and of developing a more accurate image of cause and effect. Faced with homeostatic failure, the schizophrenic adjusts his perceptions, the weak man hauls down his ideals, and the hero puts in a new furnace and insulates the house. The wisdom of the spirit consists in the knowledge of the proper proportions of these three responses—the blind eye, the struck flag, and the renewed effort.

Now let us return to the concept of discontent and its relation to social justice. The crucial distinction here—both from the point of view of the definition of social justice, and also from the point of view of its impact on the general dynamics of society—is the distinc-

tion between what might be called personal discontent on the one
hand and political discontent on the other. These are distinguished
mainly by the reactions they arouse. Personal discontent is the individual's dissatisfaction with his place in society, created by his
perception of a gap between his present condition within the framework of his society and the position which he feels he might attain
through his own efforts. Personal discontent, therefore, drives the
individual to seek a new situation within the existing framework.
It does not drive him to seek to change the framework itself. If he
is discontented with his income, he looks for a better job, he goes to
night school, or he tries to marry a rich woman. If he is discontented with his marriage, he arranges for a divorce. If he dislikes
the town where he lives, or if he cannot get along with his neighbors, he moves. Personal discontent is the muscle which moves
Adam Smith's hidden hand. It has profound impact on the dynamics of society. It diminishes one occupation and increases another.
It raises the population of one place and lowers that of another.

The political consequences of personal discontent may be pro-
digious, but they are indirect. The individual's political discontent
has direct political consequences. Political discontent is discontent
with the framework of the society in which a man operates. It may
arise because of his inability to deal with personal discontents. He
may have failed in his own efforts to improve his position: his new
job is no better than the old, the new town and the new neighbors
present all the old problems, his new wife turns out to be just as
unsatisfactory as the old one. A purely rational individual, under
these circumstances, might seek more fundamental means of assuag-
ing personal discontent, such as religion or psychoanalysis. Failing
this, however, or even after this, personal discontent may be re-
directed at the social framework. His failure to deal with his own
discontent, he argues, cannot be the result of a personal deficiency
or of ill-considered decisions. It must be the result of larger external
forces—"the system." Political discontent does not always have to
have disreputable origins, however; it may be, and frequently is, an
expression of the noblest and the most altruistic motives. Political
discontent is frequently found in persons whose personal satisfac-
tions are of the highest, but who are observant and sensitive and

who identify themselves with those who seem to be ill-treated or unhappy or unjustly served by the society—even though these others may not feel personal discontent with their treatment by society; yet even this form of political discontent may be said to arise from the individual's personal failure: his inability to do in a personal capacity what he would like for others. This failure, however, has a much more noble origin than the political discontent which arises out of merely personal failure to improve one's own position.

Whatever the sources of political discontent, its effects are frequently similar. It manifests itself in agitation for some kind of political or social change. The word *agitation,* itself, derives from a very accurate analogy. The politically discontented individual acts, as it were, to increase the Brownian movement of society, to stir up discontent in others in the hope that the increased movement of large numbers of individuals will eventually effect a change in the social vessel which holds them. Political discontent, therefore, is expressed in organization, meetings, propaganda, pamphlets, and—in its more extreme form—armed rebellion. All wars, in fact, as distinct from piracy and freebooting, must be regarded as expressions of political discontent. In some ways, the political party, the election, the letters to the editor, the pamphlets, the speeches, the processions, the sit-downs, the sit-ins, and other forms of nonviolent resistance must be regarded as an organizationally superior substitute for war. The characteristic of political discontent is struggle. This is in marked contrast to the reaction to personal discontent which is adjustment, to which such struggle as there is is merely incidental.

The concept of social justice, because it is largely irrelevant to the satisfaction of personal discontent, seems to be irrelevant to a very large area of social life. The concept of social justice is quite fundamental, however, to political discontent, for it presumably represents an ideal state of society from which the existing state is perceived as a significant divergence. It is this divergence between the existing and the ideal state of society which is perceived as the motivation for homeostatic change. Even here, however, the ideal contains a good deal more than the concept of justice. A good deal of thinking about war and peace at the moment, for instance, reflects the view that, in the present stage of military technology, it would be worthwhile paying a good deal in injustice for the establishment of a stable peace. Although war has historically been one of the ways in which men have attempted to correct what they perceive as injustices, at the present time it may be that war has become too expensive and too dangerous as a means of moving the world toward a more just order. Similarly, there may be a conflict between the claims of social justice and the desire for economic development. In certain societies, a higher rate of economic development may be achieved by riding roughshod over the more delicate issues of social justice. A similar competitive relationship may exist between justice and freedom. Freedom and justice are hard to measure, but it does seem that one may be expanded at the expense of the other. The institutions of justice inevitably limit much of the freedom of some, and some of the freedom of all. It may be argued that this limitation of the freedom of some is in the interests of greater freedom for all, but this conclusion is by no means necessary. It can easily be shown that an over-meticulous concern for justice can easily interfere with peace, order, economic growth, and freedom. An obsession with "fair" shares may inhibit the growth of the total social product, may lead to costly conflict, or may severely limit the freedom of action of the individuals in the society.

It is clear from the above that political discontent has a good many dimensions, depending on the object of discontent. If there is discontent with the anarchy of violence and war which results from the present social system, political agitation will be directed toward the establishment of world government. Discontent with the rate of economic growth may lead to agitation for a self-conscious economic program for the creation of political institutions to promote growth. Discontent with restrictions on personal liberty or with the subordinate position of a particular people or race may lead to agitation for civil liberties, national liberation or civil rights. Discontent with the distribution of the privileges and burdens of society—the feeling that some are getting more than they deserve and some are getting less—may lead to agitation for progressive income and inheritance taxes, or even for expropriation of property. These last two forms of political discontent are the most closely

allied to the concept of social justice. The concept of justice is pro-
foundly two-dimensional. It encompasses, on the one hand, what
might be called "disalienation," that is, the idea that nobody should
be alienated from the society in which he lives. This is the aspect
of justice which is reflected in the struggle for equality: the equality
of individuals before the law, the equality of racial and religious
groups in the culture as well as before the law and, in its extreme
form, equality of income. The concept here is a familistic one—
society is conceived as a great family from whose table not even the
humblest of her members shall be excluded.

The second dimension of justice is the concept of *desert*. In a just
society, each gets what he deserves, neither more nor less. It is this
concept which gives rise to a productivity theory of distribution
according to contribution, and leads to the view that he who does
not contribute to the social product does not deserve any reward
out of it. There is considerable tension between these two dimensions of justice. In general, they cannot both be satisfied. Many
sit down at the table of society who do not deserve to be there and
many eat from it who have not made any contribution. On the
strict desert theory, the young may be admitted on the grounds that
they will make a contribution in the future, and the old may be
admitted on the grounds that they have made a contribution in the
past. However, this leaves the question of the sick, the incompetent,
and the mentally deficient. We face the dilemma, therefore, that if
everyone gets his deserts, some may be driven from the table; and
if everyone comes to the table, some may not get their deserts. In
practice, this seems to be resolved by the establishment of a social
minimum as reflected, for instance, in the poor law, in social
security, and in various welfare services. The principle of desert
may come into play above this social minimum. That is to say,
society lays a modest table at which all can sup and a high table at
which the deserving can feast. This general principle can be traced
in almost all practical efforts to solve the problem.

The establishment of this principle, useful as it is, leaves a very
great many problems unsolved. It is one thing to establish the
principle of a social minimum; it is quite another thing to determine where this minimum shall be set. It may be set at the utmost

limits of Malthusian rigor—a bare table with bread and water and no propagation. It may be set higher with more sympathy, but also, perhaps, with less long-run validity as in Speenhamland and in aid-to-dependent-children. Then, above whatever minimum has been set, the principle of to each according to his deserts may be permitted to prevail. Within these limitations of the principle, however, a wide range of controversy is possible. There is an almost universal consensus that an unrestricted market economy will give the rich more than they deserve. Hence, many countries impose progressive taxation designed, not with universal success, to diminish the divergence in income between the rich and the poor. The actual schedule of taxation in any country and the rate at which it progresses seem to depend largely on historical accident. There is no clearly ideal tax schedule, and there is a strong tendency for almost any schedule, once established, to persist. There may be political discontent with existing schedules, especially among the members within the upper brackets, but it seems to be very hard to translate this discontent into political action and into legislative results. The agitation to limit tax rates in the United States to 25 per cent of income, for instance, has achieved nothing. It is very hard to make the poor and the middle class who make up the majority feel a great deal of sympathy for the worries of the rich, and hence the rich in a democratic society have little political bargaining power.

Political discontent is, then, a powerful agent of social change. It is, indeed, the principal agent of what might be called "manifest" social change, in which the course of society is deliberately directed toward a self-conscious end. The dynamics of a society cannot be understood without reference to the prevailing images of a political future. As in the case of an individual, however, the images of the future may not be realized even though they are an important element in determining it. This is even more true in the case of social dynamics than it is in the dynamics of individual behavior. We do not go anywhere unless we have a ticket, and what is written on the ticket determines where we will go. But in society, even more than in the case of the individual, what is written on the ticket is not necessarily where we end up; the latent forces in the dynamics of society often confound even the explicit plans of the politically discontented. Thus, the Christian image of a heavenly kingdom has helped to organize a good many earthly societies which have not in themselves borne much resemblance to Zion. Similarly, the communist image of a classless society has, in fact, created totalitarian and highly stratified dictatorships. The Mormon vision of a community of latter-day saints led to the establishment of the State of Utah, which maintains a level of crime and divorce comparable to other less professedly virtuous communities.

That part of political discontent which is related to ideals of social justice is sometimes a very important agent of social change, and sometimes not. A very important problem in the theory of social dynamics is to determine those circumstances under which discontent takes a personal rather than a political form and those under which political discontent aspires after social justice rather than order, growth, or freedom. There are many puzzling problems here. It cannot be assumed, for instance, that just because people are poor they will be discontented, either personally or politically. History records the existence of many peoples whose misery and exploitation have been deplorably stable and who have not given any expression of personal or political discontent. One might venture on the proposition that there is very little discontent below a certain level of poverty simply because people do not have the energy to question their lot and merely drag out an existence from day to day on their meager resources. Above this level, it may take a large improvement in conditions to diminish discontent again, as a little improvement only raises the appetite for more. Another hypothesis is that any worsening of conditions will increase discontent even if people are fairly well off to start with. The individual comes to think that he merits what he is accustomed to; hence, any worsening of his condition is a serious threat to his self-esteem. A subordinate hypothesis may then be formulated: threats to our self-esteem are the principal source of discontent, either political or personal.

A third hypothesis is that discontent, once generated, can take either a personal or a political form, depending upon the opportunities and chances of success. In a rapidly advancing society in which individuals can, with a little effort, easily participate in the general wealth, most discontent will be personal and will express itself in efforts on the part of the individual to advance his position within the existing social framework. A society, on the other hand, which is stagnant or declining will be likely to generate political discontent, for the individual who attempts to solve his problems by purely personal means will be met with considerable lack of success. This will upset his self-esteem which can only be restored by attacking the social framework.

A fourth closely related hypothesis is that if the individuals of a society perceive that political change within it is easy, whether this is in fact so or not, the discontent will be likely to take a more personal form. Thus in democracies political discontent is likely to be mild, whereas in totalitarian or autocratic societies the very suppression of political activity leads to an intensification of political discontent.

Political discontent perhaps can be subdivided further into revolutionary discontent and constitutional discontent. Constitutional discontent expresses itself, as the name implies, within the constitution of the society: it may seek to effect a change in personnel or a change in party, but not a change in the essential political system. If discontent cannot be expressed constitutionally, it will be expressed in revolutionary ways. Revolutionary discontent despairs of adequate political change within the existing constitution of society and, therefore, sets out to change the constitution itself. The degree of intensity of political discontent is important also: a mild political discontent is likely to express itself constitutionally, whereas an intense political discontent is likely to express itself in revolutionary form. The more intense the discontent, the more likely is its expression to be violent.

The next problem is to determine the mode of political discontent: that is, the circumstances under which it is likely to be directed against anarchy and war, against poverty and the failure of economic growth, against restrictions on freedom or on dignity, or against social injustice. This clearly depends upon the nature of the image of the existing society and of the divergence between this image and the ideal image. Political discontent will be directed toward those elements in society which are felt to diverge most from the ideal. If the society is orderly and war is perceived only as a peripheral activity, the problem of order and anarchy will not receive much attention. Similarly, if the society seems to be progressing satisfactorily toward greater per capita income, there will not be much pressure for general economic reform. In a society which is both orderly and progressing but in which there are large divergencies between rich and poor, or in which there is discrimination between some class or group, political discontent will mainly take the form of a demand for social justice.

This gives rise to an interesting question: is social justice an ideal which becomes important only in societies which are already orderly and progressing, or is it prominent in the political discontent even of disorderly or stagnant societies? This cannot be answered without reference to the facts of history. One suspects that there is some tendency for a dominant order of this kind: that a strong political discontent directed at social injustice is only likely to arise in those societies which are relatively orderly and progressive, and that the demands for social justice may be low in disorderly and poor societies. A possible exception to this is in those societies which have developed, as it were, a habit of political action. In such societies, if the problems of order and progress are not well solved, political action will still divert itself into the quest for justice.

The relation between discontent and action is not, itself, an invariant one. When a society has a deep interest in politics and its human energy is not "diverted" into religion, art, domesticity, or economic advancement, a small amount of political discontent may produce a disproportionate amount of political action. Under these conditions, the quest for social justice may actually prove to be inimical to that very order and progress which permitted the quest. The difficulty here is that the ideal of social justice is less easily defined than other political ideals. It is all too easy to perceive disorder or economic stagnation, and it is—perhaps—easy to perceive gross injustice. The fine definition of justice, however, is extremely difficult and there is a wide range of social states over which controversy can range. Under these circumstances, the quest for social justice may actually endanger the very order and progress which permitted it. In the struggle about the final distribution of a cake, the cake itself may be thrown to the ground and lost. One sees this even within the family where the quest for personal justice among the children not infrequently results in a bitter and quarrelsome situation in which many of the values of family life are lost. Each, in trying to get his fair share, diminishes the total that is to be divided.

We may conclude by some historical illustrations of these principles. It can be argued that from about 1880 on in the countries of northwest Europe and in the United States, the quest for social justice became a very important element in political discontent and had a profound effect on the political activities of these societies. These societies were already rich and had been—for the most part— getting richer rapidly. These societies enjoyed a high measure of internal order within this period and, until very recently, war affected them only peripherally. Constitutional rights and individual freedoms were well-developed, and the great constitutional battles against autocratic government had been won. There existed, however, a strong habit of political action and advanced institutions for legislation. It is not surprising, therefore, that the political action, on the whole, took the form of a demand for social justice which, in turn, played a dominant role in the legislative activities of these societies. In the United States, which was advancing most rapidly, discontent still took a personal rather than a political form. The American labor movement, for instance, by contrast with European labor movements, was fundamentally an expression of personal discontent. The American union, especially the craft union of the American Federation of Labor, was not an instrument to change society or even the rules of society, but an instrument by which its members bargained for better incomes. As late as the Great Depression, the American Federation of Labor was still denouncing social security. Although the socialists had some influence in the union, they were never able to dominate it. In the European democracies, however, because the class structure was more rigid and the general rate of development not as high, the opportunities for individual advancement were fewer. It is not surprising, therefore, that the discontent took a more political form and that the labor movement in Europe gave rise to the social democratic parties of later years. Yet even in Europe, the discontent generally took a constitutional rather than a revolutionary form, because of the relative lack of alienation of the mass of the people from the institutions of society. It has been the most advanced countries in Europe, with the exception of France, which have retained the institution of the monarchy. And France, perhaps, is the exception that proves the rule, for her economic development, until very recently, has been erratic, localized, and unsatisfactory.

Another interesting case study in the pathology of social justice is agricultural policy. With economic development, the proportion of the population engaged in agriculture has continually diminished so that it is now a relatively small minority in all advanced countries. In spite of this, legislative activity devoted to promoting social justice for agriculture has continually increased, and large sums are spent to subsidize what is a relatively small part of the population. Psychoanalytic roots can, perhaps, be found for this behavior: many city dwellers have rural parents, grandparents, or great-grandparents; the move to the city may reflect a rejection of rural life and rural values, which is, in a sense, a rejection of the parent, the guilt for which has been compensated for by agricultural subsidies. Part of the explanation lies in a certain constitutional lag which has resulted in gross over-representation of agricultural populations in the legislatures—for example, in the American Senate. This is not sufficient to account for the phenomenon of agricultural subsidy, however, since nearly all these subsidies required the support of city voters. The rationale of agricultural policy can only be explained by an appeal to social justice. The farm interests have made much of the fact that per capita incomes in agriculture are only about half what they are in industrial pursuits. Support, therefore, is enlisted under the concept of parity, or of equality for agriculture. Such aid to agriculture, however, has generally taken the form of price supports. These, in fact, create more injustice than they rectify, for they inevitably subsidize the rich farmer more than the poor. The poor farmers are those who have little to sell; a better price does not much better their condition, but it benefits greatly those who have a lot to sell. Agricultural price policy, then, has been an attempt to legislate social justice, the effects of which are very likely to be perverse. Nevertheless, it is the appeal to social justice which must be invoked to explain the action.

Another example of an appeal to social justice with unintended consequences is the history of the minimum wage. Minimum wage legislation is usually argued on an appeal to the principle of a social minimum. Yet the short-run effects of a minimum wage are very likely to be the pushing of considerable numbers of people below the social minimum, for many of these who previously had employment below the new minimum wage will now be unemployed. The long-run effect of a minimum wage, however, may be a technical reorganization of the affected industries which would not otherwise have taken place, and which will eventually enable them to reabsorb workers at or above the minimum wage. What is designed to be an instrument of social justice turns out to be an instrument of economic development from which social justice, as a by-product, may eventually emerge.

The essentially subordinate status of social justice as a goal of rational political discontent is illustrated by the principle that any group will find it eventually unprofitable to redistribute income toward itself at the cost even of the smallest decline in the rate of economic development. For any group which succeeds in such a redistribution there will be some year in the future beyond which it will be worse off in an absolute sense because it effected the initial redistribution in its favor. The general conclusion seems to be that social justice is something that we ought to have but that we should not want too badly, or else our craving for it will dash it from our lips and, in our eagerness to snatch it, we shall spill it.

Because many problems which appear to be problems of distribution are, in fact, problems of relative growth, there exists the danger that their treatment as problems in distribution may destroy the growth which would solve them. This may be true in large measure even of the chief problem of the world today: its division into rich countries and poor. This is a problem which can be solved, not by redistributing the riches of the rich to the poor but by making the poor productive. The rich can, and should, play an important role in the task, but the more important role must be played by the poor countries themselves: they must reorganize their societies so as to permit rapid economic development. This may seem at times like a hard and ungenerous doctrine, but it is, unfortunately, all too true. In a very real sense, justice is something that only the rich can afford. Only as the poor become rich can social justice, in any of its meanings, be established. But this is not primarily a matter of present distribution, but a matter of eventual participation in the organization and productivity of a high level society.

Lest I seem to have come out against social justice, let me add a word in its defense. There are processes in the development of a society which may be self-defeating because they violate the sense of social justice. A good example is the type of economic development in Cuba before the Castro revolution. Although it raised the per capita income of Cuba above that of any other Latin American country, it eventually destroyed itself because it violated the sense of social justice in so many people. The benefits of development were enjoyed by about twenty per cent of the people; the rest benefited little and in some cases even went backward. Discontent, which under more favorable circumstances might have found personal channels, under these conditions was channeled into purely political forms—both on the part of the peasant who felt cut off from opportunities for advancement in such a society, and on the part of his middle-class sympathizers. It remains to be seen whether the new and very different dynamic which has resulted from the revolution can, in fact, solve the problem of economic development together with the problem of social justice.

Economic development is not just a process of growth: it involves the radical reorganization of society itself. There is a stage, however, in any process of economic development at which only part of the society has been transformed. At this stage, since there are likely to be wide disparities of income between the transformed parts and the untransformed parts of the economy, development seems to have been purchased at the expense of social justice. This may be seen on a world scale today: in the eighteenth century, the per capita income in the richest country was probably not more than four or five times the per capita income of the poorest; now, the per capita income of the richest country is about forty times the per capita income of the poorest. This is not the result of exploitation but because of different rates of growth. When this disparity occurs within a society, it creates considerable strains within the social framework. The poor will inevitably become more discontented as they observe the increasing riches of the rich. If this discontent can express itself in personal terms and the process of development is such that the poor can better their condition through individual effort, political upheaval may be avoided. This was the pattern in Britain and the United States. It is also the pattern in Russia, where the Communists were able to persuade the working class to accept a sharp reduction of real income over a period of more than twenty years. This can happen only if the society can develop an ideology which prevents the poor from being alienated. If the poor are alienated, they will eventually overthrow the rich. This may bring the whole process of development to an end—as it seems to have done, for instance, in Mayan civilization. If the poor are led by the middle-class, however, the process of development could easily continue under new social forms.

These considerations underline the close relationship between the two concepts of social justice: disalienation and equality. Equality is a luxury of rich societies. If poor societies are to maintain any kind of peak achievement or civilization, they simply cannot afford it. Without sharp inequalities, we would not have had the Parthenon or the cathedrals or the great cultural achievements of any of the past civilizations. With the coming of the great revolution and what I have called post-civilization, however, equality becomes feasible as a social ideal. Equality, that is, is one of the fruits of development. On the other hand, if there is alienation, the inequality which inevitably develops in the process of development may arrest that development through political discontent. Social justice, therefore, is not a simple and a single ideal of society, but is an essential part of a great complex of social change for which some things may have to be sacrificed at times and which itself, in turn, may need at other times to be sacrificed for greater goods.

Social Justice
and the Law

PAUL A. FREUND

I

The meaning of "justice," linguistic philosophers would insist, is to be found in ordinary usage, and ordinary usage is to be found in the *Oxford English Dictionary*. The *O.E.D.*, it seems, is the Q.E.D. I have had some misgivings about the uses and usages of dictionaries. But if ordinary usage is not the be-all and end-all of meaning, perhaps it may be taken, at any rate, as the more modest members of the linguistic school suggest, as the begin-all.

Washington, where so many social concerns are focused, is filled with edifices associated with a variety of human vocations: agriculture (farmers), commerce (business), defense (land, sea, and air forces), labor (wage-earners), justice (lawyers). This survey of ordinary usage is flattering to the legal profession, but it raises a question: is justice then the concern solely of lawyers?

This identification reflects a popular fallacy, or rather a double fallacy: that the pursuit of justice is a responsibility of a professional class, and that it is centered on the process of trial and adjudication. Yet surely the suffragettes who campaigned for the women's right to vote were in as sincere a pursuit of justice as the judges who denied the right to them. The judges, to be sure, were dispensing justice as long as they denied the vote to ladies of Republican and Democratic persuasion alike; but the suffragettes were seeking justice in another and broader sense, and in another forum.

From one standpoint, justice is seen in the opposed aspects of individual and social justice. The individual voter may be treated justly if the existing rules are applied to him impartially, but the rules themselves may be inequitable and therefore unjust. This is the familiar dichotomy between internal and external standards, between honor among thieves and the dishonor of thievery. From the standpoint of its relation to law, justice is viewed in one aspect as the canon governing the judge in applying existential rules, and in another aspect, as the canon governing the legislator in altering the rules. The judge addresses himself to standards of consistency, equivalence, predictability, the legislator to fair shares, social utility, and equitable distribution.

If this is the analysis of justice in relation to law that is afforded by self-conscious ordinary usage, it stands in need of critical review. In particular, the distinction between individual and social justice, and between the judicial and the legislative function, must be examined from within the working process of the law.

II

An inscription on the wall of the Harvard Law School library taken from Justinian's *Institutes* reads: "The precepts of the law are these: To live honorably, not to injure another, to render to each his due." (*Honeste vivere, non alienum laedere, suum cuique tribuere.*) Is the last precept the only obligation referable to justice? Are the duties of good faith and due care legitimate concerns of law in society but not exactly of justice? I suggest instead that each of the precepts ought to be comprehended in justice, that each is an aspect of a more general notion.

What is this more general notion? Professor Vlastos has said that justice implies an allocation according to worth, or need, or merit, or contract. The last criterion is interesting: why contract?

Suppose that I offer a reward of one hundred dollars for the return of a lost ring, of much less intrinsic worth but of great sentimental value to me, and it is returned the next day. Is the finder entitled to the hundred dollars? He is conferring a benefit on me which I have sought and which I have publicly valued at one hundred dollars. But suppose that, completely unaware of the offer, he was moved by innate honesty to trace the ownership of the ring and return it. May I justly refuse to pay the reward? Many courts would say so, and it is hard to disagree. That element is lacking which makes a promise binding: another's legitimate expectation that the promise will be performed, an expectation usually evidenced by reliance on the promise.

Contract, Maitland somewhere remarked, is the greediest of legal categories. The law is addicted to the device of finding "implied" contracts as a way out of novel problems, and of assimilating relations—such as that of public utility and customer—to a contractual mold. The reason, I believe, is that the concept of contract is a paradigm case of justice viewed as the satisfaction of reasonable expectations. The coordinate categories of legal obligations—property and tort—are also analyzable in these terms, but contract has brought their common element close to the surface.

The history of the law of contract bears out this analysis. In early Roman law there was no generalized conception of contract: obligations arose from certain formal acts and from certain special agreements, such as loans, pledges, and partnerships. A more generalized notion produced the so-called innominate contracts, either a delivery of a thing in expectation of counterperformance (*do ut des; do ut facias*), or still more broadly the performance of an act in expectation of counterperformance (*facio ut des; facio ut facias*). Legal action to secure redress for breach of these innominate contracts was grounded on the duty of good faith and, if necessary, resort might be had to an action of *dolus* (roughly, "for deceit"). Thus the elements of the idea of contract were drawn from both property and tort.

English law, while quite independent and markedly different in detail, bears interesting resemblances. Until the fifteenth century the idea of contract was limited to the formal covenant under seal and essentially to an obligation to restore a fixed sum which had been received and was being withheld. The latter obligation was enforced through the action of debt, in which the defendant was entitled to wager of law, trial of the issue by the weight of oath-takers. The more generalized idea of contract grew up from the notion of deceit: the notion that the defendant contrived by his promise to deceive the plaintiff into parting with goods or labor. Indeed, where a debt existed though no promise had in fact been made, the judges ruled early in the sixteenth century that a promise would be conclusively presumed by which the promisee had been put off from pursuing his remedy through an action for debt; and thus the action for breach of contract, with its more rational method of trial, could supersede as well as supplement the older form. Here too contract is seen as a progeny of property and tort: the elements of both *quid pro quo* and reliance entered into its inheritance,[1] and its ancestry may flow back to the unifying idea of the satisfaction of reasonable expectations.

Is not each of Justinian's precepts an instance of the fulfillment of reasonable expectations: that a person may rely on the good faith of another, that he may expect another not to injure him carelessly or wantonly, that he may expect to receive what reasonably may be deemed to be due him? This concept of legal justice may be objected to as either tautologous or uselessly vague. But the content of reasonable expectations, although related to the positive law of the time and place, is not identical with it. The relation is one of interaction: the law is itself an educative element, as in its distrust of hearsay evidence or its prohibition of conflicts of interest and its imposition of fiduciary duties that are not always self-evident to the man of business; but reasonable expectations are more generally the ground rather than the product of law, as well as a basis for a critique of positive law and thus a ground of law in the process of becoming.

This is, to be sure, a protean concept, but its vagueness has boundaries: it is to be differentiated, on the one hand, from generosity or mercy; on the other, from will or power. Moreover, it connotes rational principles of measure and order. It was both a

---

[1] For the Roman law see R. Sohm, *Institutes of Roman Law*, Leslie transl. (Oxford, 2d ed. 1901), 397-399; W. W. Buckland, *A Textbook of Roman Law* (Cambridge, 1921), 518-523. For the English development see C. H. S. Fifoot, *History and Sources of the Common Law* (London, 1949), c. 14; S. F. C. Milsom, "Not Doing Is No Trespass," *Cambridge Law Journal*, 1954, 105-117.

classical and an Elizabethan view of justice that Shakespeare advanced in *Troilus and Cressida:*

> Observe degree, priority and place,
> Insisture, course, proportion, season, form,
> Office and custom, in all line of order;
>
> . . . .
>
> O, when degree is shaked,
> Which is the ladder of all high designs,
> The enterprise is sick!
>
> . . . .
>
> Force should be right; or rather, right and wrong,
> Between whose endless jar justice resides,
> Should lose their names, and so should justice too.

The symbol of the scales reflects the association of justice with the adjudication of adverse claims, and the process of rendering justice may be so depicted. Why not, then, reduce the fulfillment of reasonable expectations to the allocation of benefits or burdens equally according to the measure of need, or merit, or worth? But this analysis seems to drain the process of the vitality and richness that give it and its product meaning in an operational sense. The alternative criteria of equality are themselves in conflict; even when one has been selected, competing claims under it must be subjected to a degree of generalization, so that the principle of the decision may be expressed as an ethical maxim of universal conduct (to use a Kantian concept which is necessarily inconclusive in the realm of practical judgment). The immediate claimants have to be viewed, in other words, as members of classes whose contours are by no means self-evident. Moreover, even when such classes have been tentatively constructed for purposes of assessing the claims of the immediate parties, it may be found that a decision allocating benefits and burdens will produce consequences for, and affect the motivations of, still other groupings, and so the validity and sufficiency of the classes as originally constructed may be opened to question. And finally all of this is bound to be done by one or another form of human arbiter who should be mindful of his station and its duties. This whole congeries of operations cautions against a misleading reduction of the ethical problems involved in reaching judgments of social justice, even when endeavoring to hew as closely as possible to the criterion of equality.

An analysis of a case, which on its surface seems unphilosophic enough, will illustrate my meaning. The Associated Press brought suit against the International News Service to restrain the latter from taking accounts of news events published on AP bulletin boards and distributing these to member papers of the INS. The case ultimately reached the Supreme Court of the United States.[2] A majority of the Court, in what has at least the surface indicia of a progressive opinion, declared that there was a kind of property right in news belonging to him who gathered it; and for another to seize such accounts while still fresh, for his own competitive benefit, was a misappropriation, a legal wrong. There is a reasonable expectation that one will not be victimized by "piracy" or parasitism. The demands of corrective justice, it was felt by the Court's majority, required that reparation be made or at least that an undertaking be given against the repetition of the wrong.

The more interesting and significant analysis was made by Justice Brandeis in a dissenting opinion. He took the position that since news items were confessedly a peculiar kind of property, the Court had latitude in determining whether to protect it. He pointed out the interest of the community in the widest possible dissemination of information. (This counterconsideration is itself a form of equality: equality of access to knowledge and the truth.) He added that quite possibly the Associated Press made it too difficult for nonmembers to become members, through its restrictive bylaws; this in turn was a form of inequality. The Court, Justice Brandeis continued, would achieve more inclusive justice through a conditional decree, granting relief to the Associated Press only on condition that it admit INS member papers to its services on the payment of reasonable fees. In essence this solution would have converted the Associated Press into a public utility, with a duty to serve all comers at reasonable charges. But this solution would in turn give rise to a serious problem: it would promote a monopolistic position

[2] *International News Service* v. *Associated Press,* 248 U. S. 215 (1918).

of the Associated Press and would require regulation and supervision of its rates and services. In the end Justice Brandeis was
constrained to acknowledge that the courts were not equipped for
this kind of task and had no directive from Congress to embark
on it. His ultimate conclusion was that the Court should leave the
parties where it found them, lest in doing justice by halves it not
do justice at all.

There are three interrelated elements in the case. First, equality:
corrective justice from the standpoint of the Associated Press, and
distributive justice from the point of view of the members of the
INS. (Who are my peers and what is the measure of our portions?)
Secondly, community: the interest of the reading public in widely
diffused and equal access to information. (Who are my neighbors
and what are their legitimate concerns in the direction of a wider
equality?) Third, authority: the procedural aspect of a just solution.
(Who is my judge, and what are the proper dimensions of his title
to act?) A closer look at each of these elements, through the medium
of legal problems, follows.

Equality: the measure of equivalence or proportionality. The
problem is to determine the relevant peer group (to adopt a sociological barbarism), and the criteria of equivalence or proportionality.

Consider what may at first appear to be a pure problem of equality: a requirement that broadcasting networks allot free time to
political parties. "Equal time" is the maxim of justice. But what
does this signify? As between the Republican and Democratic
parties it may be taken to entail absolute equality, the same number
of hours and similar times of day. But what of small splinter parties,
Socialist or States Rights?

At least three possibilities suggest themselves. There may be
formal equality, in which the group unit, not its constituent members, is the relevant measure. Or, there may be proportional equality. Allotment according to size might be deemed an equal allocation according to achievement; but achievement may be itself a
function, in part at least, of the power to command the resources
of mass communication, the very point at issue. Or, there may be
proportional equality inversely to size, giving the smaller parties

correspondingly more time. This view might be deemed an allocation proportionate to need—but whose need? Such an allocation would diminish the time available for the major parties, leaving the mass of the electorate who are in all probability going to choose between Republicans and Democrats less informed than they would be under either of the first two solutions. Their need is consequently less satisfied. Moreover, this solution implies a choice in favor of innovation over tradition, the provocative over the familiar—a rational but disputable position. There might very possibly be side effects, such as the stimulation of small parties, with consequences for Presidential and legislative leadership, and for the efficacy of the very procedures instrumental in achieving social justice through governmental action.

All these factors are present in the problem of a just solution of a question phrased initially in terms simply of equality. To rule out side effects as not pertaining to justice but to some other values is like a dentist's claim that he has a cure for pyorrhea which will incidentally paralyze the jaw.

All three solutions are within the spectrum of justice, while some others would be clearly outside; for example, an allocation among bona fide political parties on the basis of the merit of their ideas and platforms. Although merit may be a criterion of just allocation, it is not the business of government to appraise or control the political ideas of the citizenry; it is the business of the citizenry to appraise and control the political programs of the government. It is clear then that an analysis of equality leads to consideration of equality in relation to a wider community and finally to a consideration of the problem of authority.

Consider another example, an actual case in litigation. The Railway Labor Act authorizes union shop contracts, and (let us assume) permits contributions by the union for local political causes. Certain dissident members of the union object to having their dues appropriated to political causes or candidates not of their own personal choice. This controversy bears a curious resemblance to the INS case. The union, like the Associated Press, maintains that it may justly protect itself and its members against pirates or parasites or free riders, and that the interests which the union promotes are common interests, for which all members should pay equal shares. In one respect indeed the union has a stronger case than the AP: it is an open union, to which all employees have access on payment of dues. But in another respect the dissident members have a stronger claim than the INS, for they raise the question of political equality. Who are their peers? As economic men, perhaps, all the members may be deemed equal; but as political men they are not to be equated indiscriminately with their fellow workers of the dominant persuasion. The dissident members, in order to restore their political autonomy, are obliged to pay out of a second pocket to offset the invidious contributions channeled through their union dues.

How can this conflict of two kinds of equality be resolved? Is political equality always the more fundamental? This is the philosophy, broadly speaking, of other labor and corporate legislation of Congress in relation to Federal elections. But is it the only just solution? After all, the common economic aims are hard to divorce from their realization through the political process. Moreover, the dissident employees are not forbidden to vote, to campaign, and to spend additionally as they may individually choose. Perhaps justice requires only that the union management show a genuine economic purpose in support of its political expenditures, and maintain open procedures for electing and instructing union management.

Under this analysis, then, the question of equality resolves itself into the appropriate group-categorization of the complainants: as members of a representative guild or as fully autonomous political entities. The problem arises in a lawsuit, and the claim of the plaintiffs rests on the unconstitutionality of an Act of Congress. The ultimate issue may thus become one of authority. If the legislature has taken a reasonable position and the impairment of First Amendment freedoms is oblique at best, a court might resolve the issue on the basis of its own limited function in reviewing the validity of legislation.[3]

[3] The case has now been decided, but on grounds of statutory construction, the majority of the Court not reaching the constitutional issue. *International Assoc. of Machinists* v. *Street*, U.S. Supreme Court, June 19, 1961.

Community: the interrelation of individual justice and social justice—or rather, the aspect of justice which makes it artificial and unsatisfactory to consider individual justice apart from the interests of larger groups, and the most relevant groupings. At a minimum the individuals immediately involved ought to be treated as members of classes, in recognition of the principle of universality or generality which pervades the ethical concept of justice. But more broadly, there is the question how extensive should be the inquiry into the interests of wider groups and communities. There is always the question, in other words, of the definition of the relevant society whether the immediate problem be that of so-called individual or social justice.

Consider a simple case in the law of contract. *A* promises to deliver to *B* one thousand bushels of wheat in six months at one dollar per bushel. The market price rises, at the due date it is one dollar and fifty cents, and no delivery is made. *B* waits, and after another six months, when the market price has reached two dollars, he brings suit. His claim is for one thousand dollars, the difference between what he agreed to pay and what the wheat is now worth or will cost him. The claim seems consonant with the duty of promise-keeping on a principle of *quid pro quo*. Does *B* then recover the one thousand dollars? He does not: he recovers five hundred dollars. Although *B* is wholly the innocent party, he had a duty to minimize the wrongdoer's damages by purchasing promptly from another seller, in the interest of an efficient, non-wasteful system of market exchange, which in turn has been designed to assure equivalence and reciprocity.

For a more dramatic and complex problem of community, suppose that an underdeveloped country expropriates private land holdings and declines to pay the owners the market value of the property taken. Suppose that no distinction is drawn between alien and native land owners, that the local law provides no compensation to either class. Suppose further that the government proposes to use the land for a more equitable allocation of natural resources among its indigent population. The significance of these variations on the theme of equality is brought out in an exchange of messages between the governments of Mexico and the United States in 1938 over the expropriation of Mexican land owned by Americans. The Mexican Minister of Foreign Affairs wrote to the Secretary of State:

> I wish to draw your attention very specially to the fact that the agrarian reform is not only one of the aspects of a program of social betterment attempted by a government or a political group for the purpose of trying out new doctrines, but also constitutes the fulfilling of the most important of the demands of the Mexican people, who, in the Revolutionary struggle, for the purpose of obtaining it, sacrificed the very lives of their sons. The political, social, and economic stability and the peace of Mexico depend on the land being placed anew in the hands of the countrypeople who work it; a transformation of the country, that is to say, the future of the nation, could not be halted by the impossibility of paying immediately the value of the properties belonging to a small number of foreigners who seek only a lucrative end . . . As has been stated above, there does not exist in international law any principle universally accepted by countries, nor by the writers of treatises on this subject, that would render obligatory the giving of adequate compensation for expropriation of a general or impersonal character.[4]

The Secretary of State of the United States replied:

> There is now announced by your government the astonishing theory that this treasured and cherished principle of equality, designed to protect both human and property rights, is to be invoked, not in the protection of personal rights and liberties, but as a chief ground of depriving and stripping individuals of their conceded rights. It is contended, in a word, that it is wholly justifiable to deprive an individual of his rights if all other persons are equally deprived, and if no victim is allowed to escape.

If the Secretary had been a logician, he might simply have said that equality is a necessary but not a sufficient condition of justice. The real question, however, had shifted from equality to community—to whether the claims were to be measured by the standards and expectations of the local group, or whether there is an international community whose interests and standards are relevant and even decisive.

[4] Green H. Hackworth, *Digest of International Law* (Washington, D. C.: U. S. Govt. Printing Office, 1942), III, pp. 657-60.

A related problem is found in the claims of the American Indians for compensation for the taking of their lands. Between 1863 and 1946 these claims were cognizable only through special acts of Congress conferring jurisdiction on the Court of Claims to hear particular grievances. By an act of 1946 Congress established an Indian Claims Commission, with the duty to hear and determine all claims growing out of the uncompensated taking of Indian property or the violation of Indian treaties with the Federal Government. This is a passage of President Truman's statement made in connection with the signing of the bill:[5]

> This bill makes perfectly clear what many men and women, here and abroad, have failed to recognize, that in our transactions with the Indian tribes we have at least since the Northwest Ordinance of 1787 set for ourselves the standard of fair and honorable dealings, pledging respect for all Indian property rights. Instead of confiscating Indian lands, we have purchased from the tribes that once owned this continent more than 90% of our public domain, paying them approximately $800,000,000 in the process. It would be a miracle if in the course of these dealings—the largest real estate transaction in history—we had not made some mistakes and occasionally failed to live up to the precise terms of our treaties and agreements with some 200 tribes. But we stand ready to submit all such controversies to the judgment of impartial tribunals. We stand ready to correct any mistakes we have made.

In the voluminous litigation following upon the act, probably the leading case is the claim of the Indians of California, in which liability has been established for 75,000,000 acres, comprising three-fourths of the state, at values measured as of 1851. In similar earlier proceedings, values were taken between forty cents and one dollar and twenty-five cents per acre, owed to some 37,000 Indian claimants. Liability has been established for all of Kansas and forty per cent of Nebraska, and for much of Indiana.[6] Who are to be deemed the beneficiaries of these judgments?

[5] See Felix S. Cohen, *The Legal Conscience* (New Haven: Yale University Press, 1960), p. 304. The background of the 1946 Act appears in *Hearings before the House Committee on Indian Affairs*, 79th Congress, 1st session (1945).

[6] *The New York Times*, August 12, 1959, p. 59; *ibid.*, May 3, 1959, p. 120; *ibid.*, July 14, 1959, p. 8.

The question is one of community. The victims of the failures of the Government are long since dead. Who are the rightful successors to their claims—their descendants as families or as individuals, or the tribe as a unit, or perhaps the American Indians as a single group? In fact the recoveries have inured to the tribe, whose council may determine their further distribution. In one representative case the Mountain Utes, in Colorado, collected $7,200,000 after sixteen years of litigation in the Court of Claims. The tribal council decided that half of it should go in individual grants of three thousand dollars per capita, the other half to go to the tribe for the expenses of education, health, irrigation, and the buying of new lands.[7] A relevant factor is the effect of such judgments on the likelihood of emancipation from tribal status. So long as these recoveries are possible, members of the tribe may well be inclined to remain within the community to be benefited. This in turn would forestall the development of their individual autonomy and their integration with equal legal status into the larger community. And so what at first seemed a question of equivalence, of corrective justice, involving a determination of the appropriate group to which restitution is due, takes on the problems of community: how does such a grouping affect other aspects of equality in other groupings, actual or potential?

A very different context may also be explored: the free exercise of religion in a secular state. A few states of the Union provide by law that in adoption proceedings the child shall, so far as practicable, be placed with adopting parents of the same religion as that of the child. Is such a law consonant with social justice? In terms of equality, potential adopters of a different faith will argue that they are discriminated against for no valid reason, in relation to adopters who share the child's imputed religion. On the other hand, the church will maintain that its rolls ought not to be depleted by the intervention of the state in the form of adoption proceedings; the relevant classes to be compared, the argument will run, are the church rolls with and without adoption, or perhaps the rolls of two faiths before and after adoption. If the conflict shifts to the

[7] *Ibid.,* December 2, 1956, p. 109.

question of the child's welfare, similar issues of classification appear. The potential parents will argue that the child should not be disadvantaged in relation to children born into another religious group; the church may counter that the most important element in a child's welfare is spiritual, that the most relevant group is the community of saved souls, from which the state must not remove the child. Thus, the problem entails, not merely issues of equality and the subsumption of the contending parties under various possible groups, but also issues of the relevant larger communities, secular or spiritual. There lurks, however, the further and basic issue of authority, the question of the role of the secular agencies in the fortunes of religious groups and the spiritual welfare of individuals.

It is essential therefore to consider the element of authority itself.

Authority: the appropriate person or tribunal to decide, and the appropriate procedures for decision. Lionel Trilling has remarked, in his study of E. M. Forster, that it is not enough to choose the moral result. There is, he adds, a "morality of morality." The course pursued is no less important than the goal achieved; indeed the goal cannot meaningfully be considered apart from the pursuit of it.

It is an historic principle, applied in the celebrated case of Dr. Bonham in Coke's time, that no one shall be a judge in his own cause. Equally well established is the principle that both sides shall be heard. It is a curious point of historical interest that the Fugitive Slave Law of 1850, over which a storm of moral controversy raged, violated both these procedural canons. The law fixed the compensation of the commissioners hearing the cases at ten dollars if the Negro was adjudged a runaway slave of the claimant, and at five dollars if he was not. Moreover, the law prohibited the arrested Negro from testifying in the proceedings. That these statutory vices were largely ignored in contemporary debate but would surely be a primary object of attack today is a measure of the increasing sensitivity of lawyers in America to the procedural aspects of justice. This is not to say that the great substantive issues of justice are less pressing or complex. On the contrary, it is just as those issues grow more difficult and divisive that the procedural injustices about which there can be readier consensus tend to become grounds of decision.

It is in fact in the area of procedure that the widest measure of equality, the least tolerance of classifications, is to be found. Equality before the law is a maxim of legal personality, governing access to courts and treatment before them. Alien and citizen, man and woman, pauper and prince, scoundrel and saint—all have the right to seek justice through the agency of the courts. This has been an evolutionary development, to be sure; the disabilities of married women well into the nineteenth century are a notable reminder of this. The right is, of course, an abstract one unless there is material provision to assert it effectively. This is the current stage of the process, in which the state is assuming an increased responsibility for legal aid to the indigent, some of it under the compulsion of the equal protection guarantee of the Federal Constitution.

Similarly, the right to vote is being increasingly recognized. Here too equality of participation entails a corresponding duty on the state to make it a meaningful reality, through the provision of commensurate educational opportunities. There is a positive feedback principle involved here: the increasing recognition of the right of participation gives rise to an obligation to increase the resources devoted to supporting the right.

Parenthetically, the feedback principle may be useful in approaching other, non-procedural, problems of social justice and the law; for example, the much-discussed question whether there should be a legal as well as a moral duty to go to the aid of a stranger in physical peril—whether, that is, good samaritanism ought to be more than a moral duty. In this country the law has hesitated to impose a duty of rescue unless a certain relationship to the victim exists: that the rescuer caused the peril, however innocently, or led the victim to rely on him for protection, or stood in a beneficial relation such as employer to employee or merchant to customer. Perhaps, if the law is to impose a broader social duty of rescue, it should provide correspondingly for public compensation of the rescuer in the event he is injured or suffers financial loss. This is in substance the solution adopted in Austrian law.[8]

To return to the subject of authority. Thus far we have touched on the intrinsic fairness of procedures, and the right of access and participation. Another aspect of authority is concerned with determination of the proper arbiter. In the Associated Press case, according to the dissenting judgment of Justice Brandeis, the Court was neither equipped nor authorized to undertake the kind of supervision and regulation which full justice would have required. In the union shop case, the issue of justice was reduced to the availability of fair procedures within the union organization itself and ultimately to the scope of judicial review in the light of the function allocated to the courts with respect to judging the validity of legislation.

Consider another concrete case, this one a rather familiar illustration of the relation of law and morals. A father dies and his property descends by the statutes of inheritance to his eldest son. Other members of the family allege that in fact the father was murdered by the son for the sake of the inheritance. If this allegation is true, corrective justice would require that title to the property be denied the son and placed in the next heirs of the father. That no one should profit by his own wrong at the expense of another is a convenient moral maxim that covers the case. Suppose, however, that meanwhile the property was sold by the son to an innocent purchaser. If by reason of his crime the title had never been vested in the son it would be held that it could not be transferred to the purchaser. Is the innocent purchaser, who after all paid good money for the property, to be subordinated to the innocent members of the family, who have made no expenditure at all? Furthermore, it must yet be decided whether or not a murder has actually been committed. Shall this be decided by the probate court, without the usual safeguards surrounding the defendant in a criminal trial? Perhaps an accommodation of interests could be worked out along

---

[8] See J. P. Dawson, *"Negotiorum Gestio*: The Altruistic Intermeddler," 74 *Harvard Law Review* 1073, 1121 (1961); and generally, Graham Hughes, "Criminal Omissions," 67 *Yale Law Journal* 590 (1958).

these lines: there must be a verdict of guilty in a criminal trial before the title may be attacked in the probate court; the title itself
will be unaffected, so that an innocent purchaser will be undis-
turbed; but the son will be treated as a constructive trustee of the
property or its proceeds to the extent that he retains them or holds
any assets up to the amount he received.[9]

Such a solution indicates the freedom of judges to "make" law
within limits. But what are those limits? Justice Holmes put his
view pithily when he said that judges make law interstitially, that
they are confined from molar to molecular motion. Justice Frank-
furter puts it more colloquially, saying that judges make law at
retail, legislators at wholesale.

An analogy to science may be suggestive. How far does an experiment entail a testing of scientific laws? In principle an experiment
tests not only the law which is its immediate target of inquiry but
the whole system of laws of which this one is a part.[10] Practically,
however, the subject of the test will be much more limited, unless
and until a more searching re-examination of anterior postulates
seems to be required by the puzzling nature of the result or by an
intuition that the result may be assimilated in a more satisfying way
to the larger body of knowledge.

So also with the judge. Normally, if only by reason of the need
for economy of effort, the judge is content to select and "apply"
the "rules" of law that appear to be immediately relevant.[11] This
process involves an illumination, refinement, and development of
the rules themselves in changing contexts. Nevertheless occasions
arise when this course seems less than satisfactory. The results may
no longer appear sufficiently coherent, or predictable, or just, to
warrant the judge's stopping at the immediate rules; he is impelled
to enter upon a regressive inquiry into the antecedent postulates of

[9] Various solutions are considered in Austin W. Scott, *The Law of Trusts,* 2nd
ed. (Boston, Mass.: Little, Brown, 1956), IV, sec. 492.

[10] See Morton White, *Toward Reunion in Philosophy* (Cambridge, Mass.:
Harvard University Press, 1956), pp. 255-58.

[11] I can only advert to the subtle and important question of what it means to
"apply a rule." "The notion of a principle (or maxim) of conduct and the notion
of meaningful action are *interwoven.*" Peter Winch, *The Idea of a Social Science*
(New York: Humanities Press, 1958), p. 63.

the system of rules which he is applying. The theoretical scientist is perhaps more likely than the experimentalist to undertake so searching a re-examination and to frame newer principles. In law the legislator is, for a number of reasons, freer than the judge to engage in this sort of enterprise. By directing itself to the future and making flexible its provisions, legislation can more readily mitigate the unsettling effects of a change; by employing more varied techniques of ascertaining popular and expert opinion, legislation can ground itself more confidently in the necessity for change. The importance of these factors varies greatly with the circumstances, and despite the ready cliché that legislators make the law and judges find it, these considerations are by no means always applicable or decisive.

Much of law is designed to avoid the necessity for the judge to reach what Holmes called his "can't helps," his ultimate convictions or values. The force of precedent, the close applicability of statute law, the separation of powers, legal presumptions, statutes of limitations, rules of pleading and evidence, and above all the pragmatic assessments of fact that point to one result whichever ultimate values be assumed, all enable the judge in most cases to stop short of a resort to his personal standards. When these prove unavailing, as is more likely in the case of courts of last resort at the frontiers of the law, and most likely in a supreme constitutional court, the judge necessarily resorts to his own scheme of values. It may therefore be said that the most important thing about a judge is his philosophy; and if it be dangerous for him to have one, it is at all events less dangerous than the self-deception of having none.

III

This discussion of movement in the law leads to a more general consideration of the role of law in relation to drastic social change. Continuity with the past, said Holmes, is not a duty; it is only a necessity. The law faces no greater challenge than when it must reconcile this necessity with sharply rising expectations and pressing demands for radical redistribution made in the name of justice. The role of law here is to mediate, to accommodate, to cushion.

Even the thorough recasting of the law after a social upheaval is likely to display such continuity. The French Civil Code of 1803 is a leading example: New and important popular rights were indeed conferred; but the more noteworthy feature of the Code is its continuity with legal doctrine of the past.[12]

Legal institutions have developed a variety of devices for the task of accommodation. The law, for instance, determines where the financial cost of drastic change shall fall. Here the polar positions, in legal terminology, are the "police power" of the state, which may introduce abrupt dislocations for which the community need not pay, and "eminent domain," which involves a "taking" of "property" for which compensation must be made. The essentially pragmatic content of the "police power" was described by Justice Holmes in a celebrated opinion:[13]

> When legislatures are held to be authorized to do anything considerably affecting public welfare it is covered by apologetic phrases like the police power, or the statement that the business concerned has been dedicated to a public use. The former expression is convenient, to be sure, to conciliate the mind to something that needs explanation: the fact that the constitutional requirement of compensation when property is taken cannot be pressed to its grammatical extreme; that property rights may be taken for public purposes without pay if you do not take too much; that some play must be allowed to the joints if the machine is to work. But police power is often used in a wider sense to cover, and, as I said, to apologize for the general power of the legislature to make a part of the community uncomfortable by a change.

"Taking," "property," and "public use" are sufficiently protean concepts to permit a diversified allocation of loss consequent on governmental programs of change. If the government requisitions a stock of goods for military or philanthropic purposes it must pay the owner their value; but if it forbids the shipment of goods to their intended purchaser, in order to conserve transportation facilities, there is no taking and hence no liability for loss of profits.

[12] See C. J. Friedrich, "The Ideological and Philosophical Background," in Bernard Schwartz, ed., *The Code Napoleon and the Common-law World* (New York: New York University Press, 1956) 1, 2-4; André Tunc, "The Grand Outlines of the Code," *ibid.*, 19, 33-42.

[13] Dissenting in *Tyson and Brother* v. *Banton*, 273 U. S. 418, 445-446 (1927).

Questions arise when the "property" taken is less tangible—for example, the manufacturing capacity of a plant previously serving a particular customer holding a profitable contract. The line between the "taking" and the "frustration" of a contract may be one visible more clearly to the lawyer's eye than to the economist's; it is a crude and primitive way of freeing the community from a collective burden which might retard the rate of social change or the experimental initiative of representative government.

How thorny these questions can be when they emerge on a new state's path to socialism is shown in the recent experience of India. On the basis of—some would say in the teeth of—somewhat ambiguous provisions in the constitution of 1950, the courts ruled that standards of compensation for the great estates nationalized in the land-reform program must not offend the judicial sense of fairness; and that when a local government established a publicly owned utility monopoly there was a "taking" of an existing private business which was displaced. These pronouncements were promptly overriden by constitutional amendments making the legislative standard of compensation for takings non-reviewable and emphasizing the distinction between taking and deprivation.[14]

Compensation from the public at large is not the only technique for dealing with certain losses consequent upon change. Indeed, when the government is not the immediately responsible cause of the dislocation the problem is generally approached in other ways. The law may, for instance, require minimal standards of pay and compulsory insurance, both of which are forms of social cost accounting that involve changing concepts of community. Whether it be compulsory automobile accident insurance, unemployment insurance, workmen's compensation, or overtime-wage legislation, the response is an amalgam of legal, ethical and economic standards that move away from the identification of responsibility with personal fault and toward a concept of state-wide or industrial responsibility concurrent with the common benefits of the undertaking.

---

[14] See H. C. L. Merrillat, "Compensation for the Taking of Property: A Historical Footnote to Bela Banerjee's Case," *Journal of the Indian Law Institute*, I, 375 (New Delhi, 1959); Merrillat, "C. J. Das: A Decade of Decisions on Right to Property," *ibid.*, II, p. 183 (1960).

In the community of the corporation, risks are adjusted by law among classes of investors. But the place of the employees in the corporate community has been the slowest to be defined beyond the guarantees of collective bargaining and industrial insurance. The relation of wage earners to bondholders and stockholders in the hierarchy of charges on the company's funds remains to be developed by the law. When rapid technical change is reflected in the displacement of labor, the problem becomes exigent: shall the law impose on the business this cost of a change-over, or is it to be borne by labor with such help as the whole community is prepared to afford through employment exchanges, retraining centers, work relief, and the like?

Compensation, insurance, priorities of claims are not by any means the only legal resources for accommodating change to continuity. How does the law deal with drastic changes in the price level or shifts in demand which cause deep imbalances in the economy? One way is through the renegotiation of contracts. Another is the institution of the moratorium. In the case of very severe imbalance, the law of bankruptcy may come into play. The classic legal definition of bankruptcy, an excess of liabilities over assets, has in recent times been expanded to include an inability to pay debts as they mature. Thereby the law has widened its ability to make adjustments of debts under conditions of financial stringency. The rule in bankruptcy is one of equality of sacrifice among unsecured creditors, and priorities among secured creditors according to the nature of their liens. As in the case of mergers or the introduction of labor-saving equipment, the relation of labor's claims to those of investors will be one of the pressing problems of the future.

In a more general way law must meet the dilemma of stability and redistribution through its ordinary modes of growth. In a celebrated passage Sir Henry Maine observed that the principal modes of legal development have been fictions, equity, and legislation. It is no accident that each of these is designed for the flexible adaptation of the past to the present. Fictions—the white lies of the law, Jhering called them—are the tribute that change pays to continuity. They make it possible to cope with the new without complete severance from the familiar. But they become dangerous if taken too literally. When the action of debt was usefully circumvented by the fiction of a subsequent deceitful promise to pay, it would have been unfortunate if the judges had gone on to draw the consequence that, as in the case of torts generally, an action could not be maintained after the death of the wrongdoer; luckily the tort aspect of the fiction was not allowed to control. Fictions serve the same function in law and in the life of institutions generally that word-play serves in the life of individuals: we live by metaphor, we move more rapidly by simile, and we may achieve new intellectual plateaus through the overarching abstractness of concepts.

Equity is the most flexible of legal instruments. In its characteristic sanction—the injunction—it operates prospectively by a command to desist from certain further action on pain of contempt of court, not retrospectively like a judgment at law to pay a certain sum on account of conduct already engaged in.

And the third of Maine's trinity—legislation—is itself characteristically prospective in the operation of its sanctions. Indeed, it is when legislation purports to operate retrospectively that the relations of justice and stability come into clearer focus. Under the Constitution a legislature may not impair the obligation of contracts. But individuals and groups, the courts have repeatedly declared, may not fetter the authority of the legislature over subjects otherwise within the "police power" by making contracts about them. Private interests may not by "prophetic discernment" forestall the reforming and corrective impulse of government. A brewery, for instance, need not be allowed to operate as an oasis in a dry state because it was established by public charter before the legislature introduced prohibition. A sweatshop wage is not immune from a minimum-wage law because it is embodied in a pre-existing contract.

On the other hand, if a legislature grants a perpetual tax-exemption in the charter of a private university, it will be preserved against the tax-hungry generations that would mow it down. Why the need for greater revenues should be subordinated to the contract when the need for greater sobriety or affluence is not, cannot be explained in dryly analytical terms. There is involved an implicit

judgment that the stability of a sovereign assurance is to be maintained against a general need for public funds though not against
a tide of rising moral expectations in the community.

Everyman-his-own-lawyer (who will model himself upon the most
pettifogging legal literalist) may seek to resolve these issues by defining "contract" and "impairment." What is a contract as distinct
from a mere expectancy or a mere statutory privilege? What is an
impairment of the obligation as distinct from a mere incidental or
collateral frustration of a contract or diminution in its value or
impediment to its enforceability? Questions such as these may veil,
but do not conceal, the elements of judgment entailed in valuing the
expectations of parties arising from contract or status or relationship and the expectations of the larger community.

An illustrative case is the controversy over the so-called Portal-
to-Portal Act. Congress enacted the Fair Labor Standards Act, setting minimum wages, maximum weekly hours, and requirements of
overtime pay. On the basis of the precedents, the law was undoubt-
edly effective to override employment contracts then outstanding.
"Congenital infirmity" sufficed for this. The real difficulty arose
later. In a series of decisions the Supreme Court construed the Act's
provisions to mean that in measuring the compensable workweek
of miners there must be included the time spent in traveling from
portal to portal of the mine, and not merely the time spent at the
place of actual mining. These decisions declined to regard as controlling a contrary custom or usage in the industry in connection
with wage negotiations. The effect of the decisions was to impose
on the companies a very large wage burden which they had not con-
templated either before or after the Fair Labor Standards Act.
Congress responded by passing the Portal-to-Portal Act, which
reinstated the prior understanding that custom would prevail for
purposes of computing overtime. Now it was the workers' expectations—of recent origin, perhaps, but nevertheless grounded in the
legitimacy attaching to a decision of our highest court—that were
blighted. Could Congress thus deprive the workers of these expectations? There was argument in terms of the nature of the expectations: were they contractual, or statutory, or judicially created,
or what? Were they "impaired" by a law which purported to restore

the original Congressional meaning? Judge Learned Hand, agreeing with his colleagues on the Federal Court of Appeals that the amendatory Act was constitutional, spoke in more ethical terms reminiscent of the psychological basis of Justinian's precepts of law and justice:[15]

> With the opposed interests so nearly in balance, it seems to me, not only that Congress was free to make controlling the indirect effects of the new and unexpected reading of the Fair Labor Standards Act, but that it would have been most recreant in its responsibilities if it had not done so. I trust I do not undervalue the importance of not disturbing "vested" rights; but the pith and kernel of our well-founded reluctance to do so is because otherwise the hopes of their possessors will be disappointed and they will be unable *pro tanto* to plan their future. I do not believe that that is so imperious an interest as of itself to justify sacrifices of the general interest, no matter how grave; and, in the case of an assurance so contingent and doubtful as was any that these plaintiffs could have had, it would have been shocking to allow the retention of their bonanzas to bring about the evils described in the declaration. For these reasons I think the Act was constitutional.

There is a certain irony in this episode: the legislature operating retrospectively in order to displace in turn a retrospective displacement by the judiciary; and the judiciary in the end bowing gracefully to the reallocation between stability and change.

History itself is a tension between heritage and heresy, which law in its groping way seeks to mediate. When Lincoln proposed that slaveholders be compensated for freeing their slaves he was thinking, as he characteristically did, as a lawyer. Although Franklin Roosevelt's legal training was far less likely to show in his thinking, the New Deal owed so much to the lawyers about him that the measures were at least as remarkable for their grounding in precedent as for their innovations; despite the accelerated pace and the creative novelty of combination, they owed part of their tonic effect to the shock of recognition.

[15] *Addison* v. *Huron Stevedoring Corp.*, 204 F. 2d 88, 98-99 (2nd Circuit, 1953) (concurring).

The accommodation between stability and change is representative of the ultimate task of the law—the resolution of the ambiguities and antinomies of human aspirations: personal security and moral responsibility, knowledge and privacy, triumph and fraternity.

Political Justice

The concept of political justice is obviously of practical as well
as of theoretic importance. It involves issues which have long been
and still are at the heart of political controversy: individual freedom, the rule of law, the common good, government by consent of
the governed. In this age of nuclear bombs and guided missiles it
is not an exaggeration to say that the future of mankind depends
in large part on the action taken on these issues; and this action, in
turn, will be strongly influenced by the way in which these issues
are understood and interpreted. The attempt to clarify their components and interrelations, therefore, is far more than an academic
exercise: directly at stake in the concept of political justice is a
set of ideas and ideals that are basic to the values of our civilization.

The Concept of Political Justice

The meaning of "political," like that of "law," has traditionally
varied between two extremes. One extreme is the supremely moral,
as when Aristotle (followed by Rousseau and Hegel) subsumes ethics
under politics on the ground that while every community aims at
some good, "the state, the political community, aims at the supreme
good." [1] The other extreme is the supremely amoral, as when

---

[1] Aristotle, *Politics I*, 1, 1252a 1ff. Cf. *Nicomachean Ethics* I, 2, 1094 b 5-11.

Machiavelli views politics as the use of force and fraud to obtain power and glory, or when Lasswell defines political relations as power relations, and defines power in turn as the ability to inflict "severe deprivations." [2] Between these two extremes, related at intervals to one or the other, there are two other meanings of "political." One is rhetorical, wherein "political" refers to the use of influence, persuasion, maneuvering, pressure, bargaining, and so on, to obtain an end. In this sense, to say that someone is a "smooth political operator" means that he is effective in influencing and manipulating other persons' acts and attitudes. The other meaning of "political" is the administrative, in the sense in which "academic politics" or "church politics" involves the regulation of the joint affairs of some community. Here the emphasis falls on rules and their application to a human group, without any necessary reference either to ethical ends or to rhetorical manipulation.

Each of these meanings has some justification in ordinary language and each fulfills certain purposes both of communication and of analysis. Many contemporary political scientists use a combination of the "power" and "influence" meanings. The advantages of this are clear: it enables them to view the formal institutions of government and law as causally continuous with the many other, more informal modes of power and influence in society. Political analysis can thus be sensitive to the ways in which various psychological, economic, and sociological forces operate to "coerce" men or at least to make decisions significantly affecting them. This approach is hence closely tied to a pluralistic view of politics. Yet it also has a serious disadvantage: it tends to make us regard as "political" not only the relation of a government to its citizens, but also the relations of a social lioness to would-be social climbers, of the admissions board of a medical school to its applicants, and of a criminal gang to its victims. These relations may indeed have something in common, but the differences are crucial.

It is important to note the use of "political" in a phrase such as "political unit." There is a familiar sense in which dinner parties, churches, and robber bands are not political units, while cities,

[2] See H. D. Lasswell, *Power and Personality* (New York: W. W. Norton and Co., Inc., 1948), pp. 12ff.

states, and nations are. An analysis of this sense involves not only the ideas of power, authority, and rules (which might in some way have been found in the other relations) but also the idea of supremacy. The government of a political unit has supreme power and authority in a certain territory, and this supremacy both rests on and expresses itself in rules or laws which apply to everyone in the territory and override all other rules of specific groups within it. The government is that which applies the rules and makes many of them; whether it makes all of them, and how, marks one of the differences between a constitutional and an absolute government.

The words "power" and "authority" have meanings which are intricately intermingled and differentiated. It is possible to push the meaning of "power" to the point where it joins or closely approximates such ideas as *force, compulsion, violence;* while the meaning of "authority" can be pushed in the opposite direction to signify *prestige, leadership,* and *charisma.* Yet it is possible to talk of the "powers" of the President or of Congress, meaning the authority assigned by the Constitution and by duly made laws, and of an official who arrogates to himself more "authority" than he is legally entitled to have. It is clear therefore that there is a large middle ground in which the meanings of "power" and of "authority" coincide.

In discussing political justice, it is important to avoid using a meaning of "political" that already includes justice, as, for instance, if "politics" were defined in terms of "authority," and "authority" were in turn defined in such a *de jure* way (for example, in terms of the rule of law or consent) that the requirements of justice were already contained in it. Hitler and Stalin were "political" figures as well as Roosevelt and Churchill. It is therefore more realistic to approach politics in terms of rules carrying supreme power or authority which apply to everyone in the community and carry penalties for nonobservance which are affixed in the name of the whole community. The problem of political justice, then, involves the questions of what should be the content of these rules, how they should be made and applied, to what ends, and with what limits.

It follows that although political justice does not necessarily include the whole range of social justice, it concerns those aspects which, formally at least, are ultimately decisive in any society. The exercise of political authority is conditioned by such environmental factors as customs, economics, technology, education, and moral and religious values. Yet political authority may in its turn attempt to control these same factors; it may, indeed, deal with the whole range of interpersonal relations in a society. The extent to which it ought to do so is one of the central questions of political justice.

Before these questions can be explored, the meaning of "justice" must be considered. Like "good," "justice" is used in a large variety of non-moral as well as moral contexts. To do "justice" to one's dinner is to eat it with the appreciation it deserves; to say that an actor or a ballplayer does not do himself "justice" is to imply that his performance was not up to his usual or best standard. And in moral contexts "justice," like "good," is involved in sweeping relativity; during World War II, for example, it and such apparent synonyms in other languages as *Gerechtigkeit, giustizia, spravedlivost, dharma,* or *satya* were invoked by men as unlike as Roosevelt, Hitler, Mussolini, Stalin, and Gandhi.

In view of the variety and contrariety of the objects which such political leaders declared to be just, it might be possible to conclude that "justice" has no cognitive meaning at all; that to use it is like "banging on the table" [3] to call attention to one's claims. This however, would be to confuse extension with intension, and facts with norms: that is, to confuse the fact that conflicting claims are made with the normative question of whether any of these claims is more reasonable than others. It is like saying that because "true" is attached to a large variety of statements, many of them obviously false, it follows that "true" must have only an "emotive" meaning.

To say that a statement is true is not merely to make the statement but to make a claim for it, to assert it as warranted. Similarly, to say that an act, policy, or institution is just is usually to advocate it strongly, to make a claim in emphatic support of it. I shall call this the "advocative" side of ascriptions of justice. But the plea to "temper justice with mercy" does not advocate a certain act; on the

[3] Cf. A. Ross, *On Law and Justice* (London: Stevens and Sons, 1958), p. 274.

contrary, it implies that even though the act might normally deserve support, in this case an exception should be made. There is then an aspect of "justice" which is even more basic than its advocative side: it involves the idea of something deserved because of conformity or correspondence to certain rules or principles. I shall call this the "regulative" side of ascriptions of justice. In this respect "just" is more like logical truth than like empirical truth: it connotes derivability or demonstrability from an impersonal order of principles, and also requiredness by them.[4]

The combination of these two sides of "justice" is seen in such of its synonyms as the substantive use of "right." To say that something is just is to say that some person has a right to some thing. The concept of having a right, in turn, can be explicated in accordance with the regulative aspect: for A to have a right to X means that no one ought to interfere with A's having or doing X; this "ought" derives from the moral rules or principles.

What, now, of the principles, rules, or laws themselves? Obviously to call them just cannot mean that they conform to or are derivable from other principles, for the same question could be raised about the latter. There is then a third side of ascriptions of justice: I shall call this the "normative" side. The principles of justice are ultimate moral norms which prescribe how persons (and things) have a right to be treated, both in themselves and in relation to one another. It is from such principles, which are related in various

[4] In Latin the advocative and regulative aspects of justice are seen in the etymological derivations sometimes maintained of *justum* from *jussum* ("commanded") and *jus* (the body of *"law"* which legitimates the commands and which hence is the source of *jura*, "rights"). When the regulative aspect of "justice" is combined with a meaning of "political" which unites its rhetorical sense with the idea of supremacy, the phrase "political justice" amounts to a contradiction. In such a combination, the impersonal, impartial character of justice, as found for example in the "rule of law," is negated or perverted by the "political expediency" of the sovereign regime or power-holder. For a study of this combination, which in one form goes back at least to Thrasymachus, see O. Kirchheimer, *Political Justice: The Use of Legal Procedures for Political Ends* (Princeton, N. J.: Princeton University Press, 1961). It goes without saying that the use of "political justice" in this paper is much broader; among its antecedents is Aristotle's *Nicomachean Ethics* V, 6, 1134a 25ff., although Aristotle indicates oligarchic and aristocratic as well as democratic criteria for such justice.

complex ways to conceptions of the nature of men, their capacities,
and the goals they seek, that the advocative and the regulative
sides of ascriptions of justice derive.

Disagreement on questions of justice may be advocative, regulative, or normative. Hitler and Roosevelt, for example, disagreed
in respect of the psychological attitudes which went into their
respective modes of advocacy, and in related traits of sincerity and
truthfulness. Men may agree on ultimate rules or principles but
disagree as to what follows from them. Ultimately, however, disagreements like that between Hitler and Roosevelt are normative:
they were disagreeing on the basic principles themselves of how
men ought to be treated, what rights men have both in themselves
and in relation to one another. Or, to put it in another way, while
men who are in basic disagreement about what is just have in common a certain generic meaning of "justice" (otherwise they would
not be contradicting one another), they differ as to the rules or
criteria for something to be just, for persons to have rights.

The western liberal democratic tradition, deriving in this respect
from the ancient Stoics, advances the idea of human equality as the
criterion for having rights; that is, the idea that all men as such
should in basic respects have equal rights. There has been disagreement within the tradition on the precise extent of these "basic
respects," apart from life and liberty; but in the political sphere
the emphasis has been on equality of political rights. It has often
been pointed out that equality is involved in the very idea of rules,
for rules are general prescriptions as to how to treat people, and all
cases falling under the rules ought to that extent to be treated in
the same way. There is, however, a difference between relative and
absolute equality. Equality may be relative to rules which may
themselves discriminate between men, or it may consist in men
being treated equally simply *qua* men. The western liberal democratic tradition of justice puts human equality into the very rules
or principles of human treatment.

The relation between rights and equality in this conception of
justice is the relation between the generic meaning of justice common as such to liberal democrats and their opponents, and the
further specific egalitarian criteria which differentiate democrats

from their opponents. But it is also the relation between two different components of justice, the substantive and the formal or relational. For if equality involves a relation among men, rights are the content of that relation, that is, that which is to be shared equally among men.

To a large extent it is possible to define the liberal democratic concept of justice simply by reference to the formal component, equality, so that justice would mean simply equality of treatment. Would it then be just for a ruler to deprive his subjects of their property so long as the subjects were all equally deprived? No; for such deprivation to be just, not only must the ruler himself share equality in the deprivation, but he must also allow his subjects to have a share equal to his own in the decision leading to such deprivation.

Nevertheless, a basic aspect of justice cannot be preserved unless the substantive component of rights is added to this formal component of equality. For instance, imagine a community in which all men concur in passing savagely restrictive laws which apply equally to all of them. In this case, it might be said that these men were being unjust to themselves, or were not doing themselves justice, because they were violating certain of their basic human rights, the rights of human personality.[5] Rules, then, may be unjust even if they apply to everyone equally and are approved by everyone equally. The assertion that a person is being treated justly is absolute as well as relative or comparative; it involves not only a comparison between how he is treated and how other persons are treated, but also a consideration simply of how he himself is treated as against how he ought to be treated. Justice involves not only the proportion (equality or inequality) in which things are distributed, but also what the things themselves are.[6]

The western liberal democratic tradition of justice differs from

[5] This is the point to which Locke gives a theological interpretation when he says that men are not their own property, that there are restrictions on what men can legitimately do with themselves (*Second Treatise of Civil Government*, sec. 6).
[6] Hence I disagree with Martineau when he says that the structure of justice is always triadic (*Types of Ethical Theory* [Oxford: 1898], Vol. II, p. 250). It may be dyadic as well.

other traditions on both the formal and the substantive components of justice. It holds that certain basic rights must be distributed equally, and that they must be consonant with the dignity of human personality. It would appear to be these two components that Jefferson had in mind when he wrote "that all men are created equal, that they are endowed by their Creator with certain un-alienable rights."

Is there any way of proving that these egalitarian and humanistic criteria of justice are morally superior to other criteria? To try to justify an egalitarian, non-discriminatory criterion of justice by an appeal to what would be upheld by an impartial spectator is, obviously, begging the question. For to be impartial is, by definition, to be against discrimination and for equality of treatment. Or, again, if "moral" is defined in such a way as to include impartiality or equal concern for others, then the moral superiority of these criteria of justice also follows tautologically.

Nevertheless, I think that the humanistic egalitarian criterion of justice can be defended against other criteria in at least two ways. One is by showing the incorrectness of the factual assumptions that are used to justify criteria which discriminate between people on racial or religious grounds. The second way is by a dialectical argument: if someone who opposes egalitarianism enters willingly into a discussion of the question, it is possible to show that the ethics of discussion which he thereby accepts requires of him not only traits like honesty, sincerity, and truthfulness but also mutuality or equality of consideration in the sense of treating one's interlocutors as equals; and all mature human beings are potentially such interlocutors. This is another way of saying that the rationale of honest discussion requires a recognition of the humanistic and egalitarian rules of justice.

Principles of Political Justice

If justice is equality of rights, then political justice is equality of political rights. The sphere of these political rights is that of the state with its government and laws regulating the affairs of the community. Men's political rights are the rights that they have in relation to such regulation. The problem of political justice, then, is to determine how this regulation can be moderated by the equal rights of all men.

One of the advantages of dealing with justice within the political context is that it can help avoid the utopianism which so often dogs the discussion of such moral concepts. For although it is largely within the political context that moral values such as justice, liberty, and equality can be achieved, this context also involves stringencies which drastically condition the relevance, the possibility, and the very meaning of such values. For example, the political order requires that binding decisions be made and enforced, and this entails a hierarchy of authority in which some men command and others are bound by the commands. Hence, to talk of equality and liberty without recognition of the limitations imposed by this political order is to court unrealism and irrelevance.

The principles of political justice developed in the western liberal democratic tradition have had as their aim the equalization of political rights to the extent permitted by this political context. These principles bear on two interrelated matters: the process of reaching political decisions, and the results of the process. The process involves most obviously the question of who is to have political power, and here the principle is that such power must rest on the consent of the governed. The results of the process involve the question of how political power is to be used, how the governed are to be affected by it. Here two principles have been established: one, that the results of the political process may not infringe certain basic equal rights or freedoms of each individual; the other, that the results must tend to achieve, or at least must aim at achieving, certain goods for everyone and for the community.

These three principles are interrelated in several ways. It is possible, in fact, to extend each of them so far that it can be viewed as containing the other two both definitionally and causally. The principle of consent, for example, may be held to include the principle of equal freedom in that there is no genuine consent unless men enjoy equal freedom of speech, press, and assembly. And, conversely, the principle of equal freedom may be held to include the principle of consent in that participation in the method of consent is one of the rights which governments cannot justly infringe. Or, again, the principle of equal freedom may be said to contain the principle of the common good in that governments cannot infringe the equal right of each man to have his welfare considered both in the formulation and in the outcome of policy. And, conversely, the principle of the common good may be said to contain the principle of equal freedom in that the liberties of speech, press, assembly are among the indispensable ingredients in the common good. Despite these dialectical interrelations, however, each of these principles can be explicated independently of the other two, for there are important respects in which they are distinct, and even antithetical.

The Principle of Consent

The principle of consent holds that political power is just if those who are subject to it consent or have consented to it. As the Declaration of Independence puts it, "governments are instituted among men, deriving their just powers from the consent of the governed."

The connection between political justice and consent has traditionally been upheld by at least six closely related but distinct arguments. The first proceeds through the idea of equality. In the Declaration the phrase I have quoted comes in the sentence immediately following the one in which it is asserted that "all men are created equal." A classic statement of this argument was given by the Leveller Rainborow during the English Civil War:

> Really I think that the poorest he that is in England hath a life to live as the greatest he; and therefore truly, Sir, I think it is clear, that every man that is to live under a government ought first by his own consent to put himself under that government; and I do think that the poorest man in England is not at all bound to that government that he hath not had a voice to put himself under.[7]

Since all men are equal in dignity or worth, the only ground on which one man can justly exert power over another is that the latter

[7] *The Clarke Papers,* ed. C. H. Firth (London: Camden Society, 1891), Clarendon Press, Vol. I, p. 301.

consents. By this argument, all attempts to justify political authority by the inherent superiority of some men over others, or by any other kind of "natural" difference of status, are ruled out.

A second argument appeals to the idea of freedom or autonomy. If a man has consented to government, then the government's acts become his own acts, and hence he in effect governs himself and is politically free. Consent thus furnishes the answer to what Rousseau called the problem of *droit politique*, the problem of how "to find a form of association . . . in which each person, while uniting himself with all, may still obey himself alone and remain as free as before." [8]

A third argument is based on the idea of non-injury. There is a famous maxim of private law that he who consents to an act is not wronged by it (*volenti non fit injuria*). Consent, therefore, makes just the coercive and punitive power of government.[9]

A fourth argument holds that justice consists, at least in part, in distributing rights and duties to persons in accordance with the promises they have made. If, then, men have promised or consented to obey government, they are obligated to obey it, and consequently the government can justly exact such obedience.

A fifth argument appeals to the idea of purpose. In the traditional governmental version of the social contract theory, subjects promise to obey their ruler because the ruler has in turn taken on the obligation of protecting the subjects. The subjects' consent thus involves a *quid pro quo*, so that the original natural equality among men is succeeded by a more complicated equality in which, by the ruler's fulfilling the purpose of his authority, the rights and duties of the ruler and the subjects reciprocally limit and balance one another.

The sixth argument involves other common goods besides protection. It has been held that only if the government is subject to popular consent is there assurance that political power will be used for the interest of the whole community and not perverted to the selfish interests of the ruling group.

[8] Rousseau, *Social Contract*, I, vi.
[9] For this argument, see Kant, *Philosophy of Law*, par. 46, trans. W. Hastie, (Edinburgh, T. & T. Clark, 1887), p. 166. Cf. the critical remarks of J. S. Mill, *Utilitarianism*, ch. V (Everyman edition, p. 52).

These six arguments of traditional consent theory are obviously not all on the same level; they may in various ways be extended as well as reduced to one another. But there emerges a common conclusion from them: consent is the necessary condition of political obligation. This conclusion is presented clearly in such famous phrases of John Locke as that "no one can be . . . subjected to the political power of another without his own consent," "that which acts any community being only the consent of the individuals of it," "the supreme power cannot take from any man any part of his property without his own consent." [10] What Locke is saying can be expressed by the hypothetical statement: *If there is political obligation, then there must be consent.* This doctrine involves two difficulties, one of which is anarchy. It arises from the connection between the antecedent and the consequent in the hypothetical statement: if consent is the necessary condition of political obligation, then such obligation ceases whenever consent is withdrawn. Whatever else government may involve, it requires at least the potential coercion or compulsion of its subjects to obey its laws or other commands. But if no act of government is legitimate or just unless the individual to whom it is directed consents to it, then compulsion to obey is obviously ruled out, and government is replaced by anarchy.

The second basic difficulty of the consent theory is unrealism, which involves the consequent of the hypothetical statement given above: *there must be consent.* As Hume, Bentham, and many other critics have pointed out, the idea that political society rests on a contract in which subjects consent to be governed is a fiction. If it be replied that such consent is not to be viewed as a real historical event but only as an ideal which must somehow be fulfilled if authority is to be legitimate,[11] we must still ask about the kinds of conditions which must be met if the ideal is to be fulfilled or even approached.

To understand the further components of these difficulties, as well as the various attempts to cope with them, three questions

---

[10] *Second Treatise of Civil Government,* secs. 95, 96, 119, 138.

[11] Cf. Kant, *Principles of Political Right,* in Kant's *Principles of Politics,* trans. W. Hastie (Edinburgh: Clark, 1891), pp. 46-47.

about the principle of consent must be distinguished. Who is it that must give consent? To what must the consent be given? In what must the giving of consent consist? I shall call these, respectively, questions about the subject of consent, the object of consent, and the nature of consent. Traditional consent theories have often begun from one extreme answer to these questions and then, seeing the unacceptability of this extreme, they have tended to go part or all of the way to the opposite extreme.

According to one extreme answer, the subject who must give consent to political power before it can be just is always each individual who is to be subjected to it; the object to which he must give consent is each particular exercise of political authority; and the nature of the consent is explicit agreement or authorization or permission given by the subject to the ruler or the agent of political power. I call this the *occurrence* version because it views "consent" as an occurrence word [12] signifying a particular occurrence caused by a particular individual in respect of a particular act of political authority.

It is difficult to know whether anyone has ever upheld exactly this version of the consent principle, but some of the statements of John Locke can lend themselves to such an interpretation. The dangers of anarchy and of unrealism are obvious.

The opposite extreme version of the consent principle holds that the subject who must give consent is no longer each individual but rather a whole people; the object to which consent must be given is no longer each particular exercise of political authority but rather political authority as such, as represented, perhaps, in some primordial constitution from which derive all the laws and all acts of political authority; and most important of all, the nature of the consent which must be given is no longer explicit agreement or authorization but rather some vague, general consensus which amounts to a tacit, irrevocable acquiescence. I call this the *generic dispositional* version of the consent principle because it views consent not as a particular act occurring at a particular time but as a long-range habit or custom of obedience which can be attributed to

---

[12] For this, and also for "dispositional" words referred to subsequently, cf. G. Ryle, *The Concept of Mind* (London: Hutchinson, 1949), Ch. V.

a whole population, or at least the bulk of it, *en bloc,* despite or perhaps because of its passivity in accepting the regime. So long as a given population lives under a given law and government it is presumed to consent to them, and any act of resistance is assumed to be counter to the wishes and consent, *i.e.,* the acquiescence, of the overwhelming majority, as exhibited in its acceptance of the authority in question.

Now it is obvious that, just as the occurrence version of the consent principle carries the direct risk of anarchy, so the generic dispositional version can readily lead to, or at least is consistent with, tyranny. Most tyrannies, including those of recent times, have claimed to rest on consent in at least this dispositional sense.[13] John Locke recognized not only that there are relatively few cases in which men give any explicit expression of consent to political authority, but also that to make political authority depend upon such explicit consent to each exercise of authority would annihilate political obligation: "What new engagement [would a man have] if he were no farther tied by any decrees of the society, than he himself thought fit, and did actually consent to? This would be still as great a liberty as he himself had before his compact . . ." To avoid this anarchic extreme, Locke declared that the consent which is required to legitimate political authority may be "tacit" as well as express. He defined "tacit consent" as follows: "Every man that has any possession or enjoyment of any part of the dominions of any government does thereby give his tacit consent,

---

[13] Cf. the satirical comment of Bentham, *Truth versus Ashhurst (Works,* ed. Bowring [Edinburgh, 1843], Vol. V, p. 235):

> *Ashhurst.*—Happily for us, we are not bound by any laws but such as are ordained by the virtual consent of the whole kingdom.
>
> *Truth.*—Virtual, Mr. Justice?—what does that mean? real or imaginary? By none, do you mean, but such as are ordained by the *real* consent of the whole kingdom? The whole kingdom knows the contrary. Is the consent, then, an imaginary one only? A fine thing indeed to boast of!
>
> "Happily for you," said Muley Ishmael once to the people of Morocco, "Happily for you, you are bound by no laws but what have your virtual consent: for they are all made by your virtual representative, and I am he."

and is as far forth obliged to obedience to the laws of that government during such enjoyment as anyone under it;" so, Locke con-
cluded, ". . . in effect [such tacit consent] reaches as far as the
very being of anyone within the territories of that government." [14]
This means that so long as one lives under a government one tacitly
consents to it. It need hardly be pointed out that on this definition
even a gangster who flouts the laws of a state gives tacit consent
to it.[15] And it is also clear that this version of consent marks a
sharp departure from Locke's original model of each individual
actively agreeing to the political authority which is exercised over
him and only by that agreement making the authority legitimate or
just.

A government might be said to rule with the tacit consent of its
subjects if by and large they obey its laws and seem to do so
willingly, if they seem in general contented and show few if any
signs of being rebellious, so that the government does not have to
be unduly harsh or repressive.[16] In such a context, "consent" is a
dispositional rather than an occurrence word: to say that men consent is not to say that they have ever explicitly promised or agreed
to obey the government but rather that if they were asked so to
agree, they would do so. There is, I think, a real difference between
tacit consent as thus understood and the lawlessness or rebellious-
ness that would be compatible with Locke's definition of it. Nevertheless, such consent is still only passive; it might mark a primitive
tribal regime and many others that we would not ordinarily think
of as governing by the consent of the governed. Government by
consent, as a democratic concept, must involve much more than
this.

It might seem, then, that a proper interpretation of the principle
of consent must lie somewhere between the occurrence version

[14] *Second Treatise of Civil Government*, secs. 97, 119. Cf. Rousseau, *Social Con-*
tract, IV, ii.

[15] Cf. J. P. Plamenatz, *Consent, Freedom, and Political Obligation* (London:
Oxford University Press, 1938), p. 7; J. W. Gough, *John Locke's Political Philoso-*
phy (Oxford: The Clarendon Press, 1950), p. 64.

[16] Something like this is implied in such a late medieval version of *tacitus*
consensus as that found in Coluccio Salutati, *De Tyranno*, II, 8 (quoted in
M. V. Clarke, *The Medieval City State* [London: Methuen Co., Ltd., 1926], p. 140,
n. 1).

and the generic dispositional version. The subject of consent could be the majority or some greater or lesser percentage of the whole population, and various qualitative specifications could also be added, including not only adulthood, sanity, non-criminality, but also some degree of property or education. The nature of consent could vary from direct participation in making laws to electing delegates or representatives; it could be alterable or unalterable, and expressible in various ways. The object of consent could be the government, or the laws, or the basic constitution, or some combination or selection from among these. Obviously some of these alternatives are more democratic than others. Yet, unless certain basic qualifications are recognized any alternative version will be subject to the same difficulties of anarchy and unrealism.

It is essential, first, to distinguish between general and specific objects of consent and of political obligation. By the general object, I mean government as such. This involves the general question: Why should there be any government at all? Why should there be any political obligation at all? This was the question for which not only Locke and Rousseau, but even Hobbes, ultimately adduced consent.[17] Their assumption was that only consent could justify the transition from the apolitical state of nature to the civil state or commonwealth. This assumption, with its concomitant requirement of unanimity and its consequent difficulties of anarchy and unrealism, has hampered the theory of consent ever since. Democratic political philosophers have felt that unless political authority as such could be shown to rest on the consent of each individual subject to it, it could not be legitimate in respect of that individual. And it has also meant that theorists have been able to find no other tenable meaning for "government by consent" than this occurrence version whereby the subject of consent is each individual and the nature of consent is some kind of explicit agreement.[18]

[17] Hobbes, *Leviathan,* Chs. XVII, XVIII; Locke, *Second Treatise of Civil Government,* sec. 95; Rousseau, *Social Contract,* I, vi; IV, ii.

[18] Cf. J. Tussman, *Obligation and the Body Politic* (New York: Oxford University Press, 1960), pp. 32-37; Plamenatz, *op. cit.,* pp. 23-24; Gough, *op. cit.,* p. 71; A. C. Ewing, *The Individual, the State, and World Government* (New York: The Macmillan Company, 1947), pp. 114-15. A. Meiklejohn, *Free Speech and Its Relation to Self-Government* (New York: Harper & Bros., 1948), pp. 9-16.

In fact, however, in addition to the anarchic and unrealistic consequences that we have already noted, there are at least two reasons why consent is not required to justify government as such. First, a primordial or generalized consent would not serve to distinguish one kind of government from another. As the example of Hobbes indicates, the appeal to consent to justify government as such can justify a totalitarian government as much as any other kind; for a totalitarian government is still a government. It is significant that not only Hobbes but also Locke and Rousseau drop unanimous consent from further consideration as soon as they have used it to justify the institution of the political community and government as such, and they assign to the majority the effective choice of and consent to the specific government.[19] They therefore regard unanimous consent only as the basis of the primordial constitution, but not as limiting or otherwise controlling the specific institutions of actual government. Since, however, the primordial constitution (the "social compact") exerts no control over the specific kind of existing government, the original unanimous consent does not provide a basis to differentiate one kind of government from another.

A second reason why consent is not required to justify government as such is that the necessity for having government is manifestly demonstrable in other ways. As nearly all political philosophers agree, human life itself is impossible without government. To see the imperative need of government, one need only imagine, as Hobbes did, what life would be like without it. Strictly speaking, then, Hobbes should not have adduced consent as an additional justification for government. The question whether there should be any government at all is even less dependent on consent than the question whether men should live, for while each man's living or not living might be ultimately regarded as his personal or private affair, the question whether or not there should be government is intrinsically an interpersonal matter and as such should not be subject to a purely individual consent or decision.

The real question for consent theory, then, involves not the general but the specific object: not whether there should be any

---

[19] Hobbes, *Leviathan*, Ch. 18 (*init.*); Locke, *Second Treatise*, secs. 96-98; Rousseau, *Social Contract*, IV, ii.

government at all, but what kind of government there should be, who should have the authority to govern. The question of political obligation to which consent provides the answer is not, Why should one obey any government at all? but rather, Which government should one obey?

Here again, however, tradition has established a sequence of replies which opens the way to the difficulties of unrealism and anarchy.

The first step is to answer the question of the specific object of consent by means of the subject and the nature of consent. One is obligated to obey that government to which the majority has consented through election. But, strictly speaking, such consent justifies only the majority's obligation to obey. The minority which voted against the government or those who did not vote at all—on what does their political obligation rest? Here comes a second answer: their obligation rests on their having consented to the general constitutional rules which determine that it shall be by majority vote that the specific governmental authority is allocated. But now there arises again the question of the nature of this consent by the minority and the others. When did they consent, and how? For immigrants, of course, this question may be answered by referring to an oath of allegiance taken at the time of securing citizenship. But what of those who were not immigrants, and generally of those who have taken no oath? At this point we are thrust back to tacit consent.

This well-trodden path is a misconceived blind alley from the start. The root misconception lies not in the appeal to consent as such but in the way in which the subject, the object, and the nature of consent are viewed in relation to one another and to political obligation. Even if they avoid the extreme occurrence version of consent theory, political philosophers still retain that aspect of it which views the relation between the three components of consent in a completely determinate fashion. That is, consent is viewed as a determinate act or occurrence on the part of determinate persons, and its object is some determinate phase of political authority. There arise therefore the problems of locating and describing this occurrence, and of so relating it to its object that in the absence of the occurrence the object has no authority to compel obedience, nor has its subject any obligation to give obedience.

This, however, is not that we mean when we say that the United States and Great Britain have, and the Soviet Union and Communist China do not have, governments that rest on the consent of the governed. It is not a question of being able to find in the former case, and not in the latter, acts of consent that stand in one-to-one relations to determinate citizens or "subjects" on the one hand and political obligations on the other, and that hence serve to relate the citizen to his government by ties of obligation. Government by consent means, rather, that the specific holders of political authority are not independent variables so far as their authority is concerned but are dependent on the votes of the electorate. This entails that the government, as a matter of constitutional requirement, is regularly subjected to a process which passes judgment on it and may transfer its authority to other hands. The right of dissent is thus a basic part of the method of consent. The process culminates in an election, but it also includes free discussion and criticism of the government's policies, and competition for votes among different parties. The government is thus subjected to the various pressures of various groups within the electorate, and the election, which may be viewed as the culmination of those pressures, determines who is to occupy governmental office in the subsequent period. The government's right to govern depends finally on its winning the election by the constitutionally required majority or plurality of votes.

This process, so familiar to the western democracies but so often lacking in other parts of the world, constitutes the method of consent. And it is this method which, according to the liberal democratic tradition, legitimates political authority and political obligation. If the method is subverted or overridden, then there may still be an obligation on other grounds to obey government as such, but the specific government which has been the instrument or the result of this subversion has no claim to allegiance so far as the principle of consent is concerned.

From this, it is clear how the elucidation of the principle of consent by the method of consent provides an answer to the traditional theory's difficulties of anarchy and unrealism. The consent which is a necessary condition of political obligation is not primarily the consent of determinate individuals occurring at specifiable times; it is rather the maintenance of a method which leaves open to every sane, non-criminal adult the opportunity to discuss, criticize, and vote for or against the government. The individual is obligated to obey the government whether he personally utilizes his opportunity or not, and whether he votes for the government or against it. And if he is refused the right to vote, then, so far as the principle of consent is concerned (and apart from all other considerations justifying the maintenance of government), he is still obligated to obey if the government through its various arms is palpably taking steps to remove the obstacles that have been wrongly put in the way of his participation in the method.

The word "consent," then, in the method of consent is directly neither an occurrence word nor a disposition word in that form where it would mean "if one were asked, one would consent." It is rather a potentiality or opportunity word; its meaning is that one can participate if one chooses to do so. It is also a social or collective word rather than an individual word; for such consent to exist means not that certain acts occur in determinate individuals but rather that certain institutional arrangements exist in a community as a whole. To be sure, if amid such communal arrangements there occurred no individual acts of consent at all, we should be justified in suspecting that something was wrong. In this respect, the relation of consent as a potentiality to consent as an actual occurrence is different from the relation of the solubility of sugar in water as a disposition to the actual dissolution of sugar in water. If for the next fifty years no piece of sugar were placed in water and hence dissolved, we should still be justified in maintaining that sugar is soluble in water: the existence of the disposition is not affected by whether it is actualized or not. But if during the next decade no person in the United States or Great Britain were actually to express his consent or dissent by voting or other such explicit behavior, it would be justifiable to think that the potentiality or opportunity for consenting or dissenting was itself absent. When the method of consent is operative, however, such extreme cases do not occur.

The model of the traditional version of consent theory may lead to dissatisfaction with this explication of the consent principle. What is the justification for the method of consent itself? Why is an individual obligated to abide by its results, *i.e.*, to obey the government which is set up by the working of the method? There is a temptation to say that he is not thus obligated unless he has consented to the method—and this gives rise again to the difficulties of unrealism and anarchy.

There are several answers to this question of justification. The method of consent combines and safeguards the joint values of freedom and order as no other method does. It provides a check on the power of government which protects the rights of the electorate more effectively than does any other method. It does more justice to man's potential rationality than does any other method, for it gives all men the opportunity to participate in reasoned discussion of the problems of their society and to make this discussion effective in terms of political control.

It may, however, be objected that since consent has been justified by other values than consent itself, it has been removed from the status of principle. There is a sense in which this is true, but I see nothing fatal in it. The problems of political justice are too complex to be reducible to any one principle. There is, however, another answer to this objection. If the method of consent is not accepted as its own justification, and some kind of further tacit or express consent, on the part of each individual, is looked to for its justification, the prospect may well be infinite regress. For, on the same ground on which the latter justification is demanded, the general rule that individual consent shall justify the method of consent will itself stand in need of a still further justification by individual consent. And there seems no way to stop this.

What, however, if an individual dissents not only from the specific government but from the whole constitutional structure which provides the method of consent as the way of appointing the government? The method of consent is a method which operates within a given society as a condition of political justice and obligation. But if the condition is rejected, then it would seem that voluntary removal from the society is the only justifiable recourse.

I have been dealing with the principle of consent as a principle of political justice; I have not been concerned with the various sociological and other factors which condition its actual operation. The many studies of voting, including the "engineering of consent" and other forms of persuasion, are important correctives of a too hasty idealization of the democratic process. Unrealism is as much to be avoided in describing the method of consent at work as in distinguishing it from traditional versions of consent theory. Yet all the aberrations in its actual operation must be observed in their context. The context includes the virtues of openness and pluralism which, by their very nature, can eventuate in different directions. These virtues make possible both a security and a self-correction denied to other methods of allocating political authority.

One of the most pressing problems in the contemporary world is the relevance and applicability of the method of consent in those many nations which lack democratic traditions. For the most part, these are nations which also lack the economic, educational, and other prerequisites to successful operation of the method.[20] Yet this does not remove the possibility that, once these prerequisites are achieved, the method will be as much a condition of political justice for such nations as it is for those of the west. There is another prerequisite, however, which is also hard to achieve. It has often been stressed that democracy requires a broad consensus among the people on certain basic values.

> Prior to politics, beneath it, enveloping it, restricting it, conditioning it, is the underlying consensus on policy that usually exists in the society among a predominant portion of the politically active members. Without such a consensus no democratic system would long survive the endless irritations and frustrations of elections and party competition. With such a consensus the disputes over policy alternatives are nearly always disputes over a set of alternatives that have already been winnowed down to those within the broad area of basic agreement.[21]

[20] Cf. S. M. Lipset, *Political Man* (New York: Doubleday and Co., Inc., 1960).
[21] R. A. Dahl, *A Preface to Democratic Theory* (Chicago: University of Chicago Press, 1956), pp. 132-133.

Consensus is not, however, the same thing as consent as found in the method of consent. It comes much closer to the concept of tacit consent. There can be many kinds of consensus: caste-ridden societies and states ruled by absolute monarchs as well as democracies have their consensus. Nor is a democratic consensus a sufficient condition of the method of consent; the latter requires formal, constitutional means of allowing public discussion to eventuate in voting whereby the majority determines who is to hold political authority. A democratic consensus, however, may well be a necessary condition for the operation of the method of consent. Yet the converse is also possible: that, at least within certain limits, the existence of the method of consent, with its opportunities for discussion of all points of view, is a necessary condition of a democratic consensus. In any case, the most important component in such a consensus is agreement on the method of consent itself: agreement that, regardless of what divides men, they will always abide by the method of consent to settle their differences. Such an agreement may consequently embody moral values such as mutual respect which both foster and are fostered by the method of consent as the institutional process of reaching decisions concerning the rules and rulers of the community.

The Principle of Equal Freedom

The method of consent includes discussion, criticism, persuasion, competition, but it eventuates in majority decision. This fact involves the possibility of serious tension because of the difference between method and result, process and decision. The method is open, fluid, free; and all have an equal right to participate in it. The decision itself, however, is closed in that it settles, for a while at least, the questions at issue. It limits freedom inasmuch as it fixes one alternative as authoritative and removes the others from contention. It is a political decision not only in respect of the processes which precede it but also in respect of the coerciveness which attends its conclusion. It sets up a government whose laws are binding on all the members of the society, with penalties for nonobservance.

This tension raises the question: are there any restrictions as to the objects with which majority rule can justly deal or as to the governmental procedures which it can justly permit? For example, to what extent, if any, may majority vote pass laws about, or otherwise attempt to regulate or control, speech, religion, the press, education, marriage, the family, the arts and sciences, monetary savings, wages and salaries, choice of occupation? And may the government operate by bills of attainder or *ex post facto* laws? The demand for limits on majority rule and on the powers of government in general creates a new dimension of political justice, concerned not with the question of who should govern or from what source should political power be derived, but rather with the question of the just limits of power, no matter by whom exercised or from where derived. While the principle of consent can itself be viewed as setting limits to political power, in that no power is just if it does not emerge from the method of consent, the question of limits which we are now considering concerns not primarily the source from which power must be derived but rather the content of the exercise of power, however it may be derived. If the doctrine of majority rule has traditionally gone by the name of *democracy*, the doctrines advocating limits as to the objects and the methods of all governments, including democracies, have gone by the names, respectively, of *liberalism* and of *constitutionalism*.

It is important to distinguish the factual, empirical question of what democratic majorities have done or are likely to do in regard to individual liberties and governmental procedures, from the logical question about the relation between the concept of democracy as thus defined and the concepts of liberalism and constitutionalism. To say that the concept of democracy as government by majority rule does not, as such, include the concepts of liberalism and constitutionalism as setting limits to the objects or methods of governmental control is by no means the same as to say that democracies have no concern for or that they have violated or will necessarily violate the limits set by these concepts, nor that there must be explicit political or legal devices to guarantee that government does not violate the limits in question. It is not even necessarily to deny that democracy in the sense of majority rule, with the self-corrective operation of the method of consent, may be the best guarantee of liberalism and constitutionalism. It is to say only that the criteria of political justice which enter into the concept of democracy as majority rule deriving from the method of consent are distinct from the criteria which enter into the concepts of liberalism and constitutionalism.

We might, however, try to build the liberal and constitutionalist limits into the very concept of majority-rule democracy. This would be to say that there is no other *meaning* for an act or limitation of political power to be just except that it has been sanctioned by the method of consent. Here the justice of the limits would be defined by the justice of the source or method.

The argument for such a definition could take a simple form: that consent is both the necessary and the sufficient condition for just political power, so that there can be no transgression of the just limits of power if the power has been consented to. This would be to deny that there is, or can be, any criterion of political justice other than consent. However, it is not self-contradictory to say (as the doctrine of inalienable rights implies) that although a man consented to the restriction of his basic rights, he had no right to do so. Self-enslavement and suicide are examples of this. Moreover, the question of just limits involves not merely personal or individual consent to a particular act but the whole political context envisaging coercive measures for a large population. Majority consent in this context therefore comprises the coercion or restraint of many persons who have not themselves consented to the measure in question.

There is, however, a more complex defense of the definition of the just limits of political power in terms of the source of power. The argument is that what makes majority-rule democracy just is not simply the majority decision itself but rather the whole method of consent out of which it emerges. This method already involves certain basic freedoms for all men equally, and in general equal possibility of access to political authority and influence. Now this same libertarian and egalitarian context supplies the necessary precondition not only of the process leading to political authority but also of the operation of such authority. That is, political authority is not just if its operation violates or restricts the freedoms and equalities of that method of consent which is the condition of justly acquiring the right of governmental power. This is in part a specific form of the general principle that the morality of an end is limited by the morality of the means or method leading to the end.

While such a line of argument might go some way toward including the concepts of liberalism and constitutionalism within the concept of democracy, it would not go as far as the conditions of justice on which the liberal and constitutionalist traditions have insisted. The emphasis of these traditions is on drawing a line between the powers of government and the liberties of the individuals, but the emphasis of democracy is on assimilating government and people by some such relation as that of principal and agent in virtue of the people's having consented to the authority of government. In this respect, the method of consent appears not as limiting government, but rather as legitimating the authority of government. Hence the question remains open as to the limits of governmental authority in respect of the individual. Even if, moreover, the method of consent is viewed as limiting the operation of government, the sphere of what is thus limited or exempted from governmental control does not include the whole range for which liberalism has stood. The limitations justified by the method of consent would exempt from governmental control such acts relevant to political action as speech and assembly; but is there anything in the method as such that would justify limiting the authority of government with respect to the family, property, choice of occupation, the arts, and the whole range of other activities not directly involved in the political pursuits of the method of consent? From the standpoint of the method of consent such limitations would be justified only if the majority decided in favor of them. But the point of the liberal and constitutionalist positions is that there are certain limits beyond which political power cannot justly go regardless of consent or other considerations of the source of power. It might be possible, of course, to extend the method of consent into a generalized libertarian position. But this would be an extension; it is not entailed by what is directly contained in the method of consent as such.

The criterion of justice found in the principle of consent can, however, be assimilated to that which is relevant to the just limitation of political authority. For just as the principle of consent involves that men are equally free in respect of participating in the process which determines who is to have political authority, so the concept of equal freedom may be held to apply likewise to the question of the limits of political authority. In each of these two applications "freedom" means absence of external restraint; but whereas in the former case this refers to men's autonomy or self-determination in controlling the government under which they must live by participating in the method of consent, in the latter case it refers to men's ability to determine their actions without any restraint from the government. These two applications of freedom may be viewed as marking out respectively what Benjamin Constant distinguished as the "liberty of the ancients" and the "liberty of the moderns," the former consisting in "active and enduring participation in the collective power" and the latter consisting in "the peaceful enjoyment of private independence" and the "guarantees accorded by institutions to these enjoyments." [22]

The concept of equal freedom may be viewed in such fashion that while each of its components applies both to liberalism and to constitutionalism, the concept of freedom applies more peculiarly to liberalism and the concept of equality to constitutionalism. For liberalism stresses the exemption of the individual from governmental restraints, while constitutionalism stresses the formal framework of the rule of law whereby men are entitled to equality before the law and to equal protection by the laws.

There still remains, of course, the question of how the principle of equal freedom serves to delimit the area of freedom. It is all very well to say that freedom should be maximized; but, as is recognized

---

[22] *De la liberté des anciens comparée à celle des modernes* in *Oeuvres politiques de Benjamin Constant,* ed. C. Louandre (Paris: Charpentier, 1874), pp. 268-69. Cf. Constant's discussion of the limits of popular sovereignty in *De la souveraineté du peuple (ibid.,* pp. 4-5).

by even such an emphatic libertarian as J. S. Mill, "all that makes existence valuable to any one, depends on the enforcement of restraints upon the actions of other people." [23] This is another way of making Hobbes' point about the state of nature: without restraints of the kind formalized by positive law and government human life becomes impossible. But what is the just extent of such restraints? Is there any principle which determines the area within which men may be free to do as they wish, without restraint from any external source? I wish now to consider some of the chief attempts to answer this question through the principle of equal freedom.

Consider the following statements:

(1) It is a law of nature "that a man be . . . contented with so much liberty against other men, as he would allow other men against himself." (Hobbes) [24]

(2) "Every man is free to do that which he wills, provided he infringes not the equal freedom of any other man." (Spencer) [25]

(3) "Everyone is entitled to seek his own happiness in the way that seems to him best, if he does not infringe the liberty of others in striving after a similar end for themselves when their liberty is capable of consisting with the right of liberty in all other men according to possible universal laws." (Kant)[26]

(4) "The only freedom which deserves the name is that of pursuing our own good in our own way, so long as we do not attempt to deprive others of theirs, or impede their efforts to obtain it." (J. S. Mill) [27]

---

[23] *On Liberty*, Ch. I (Everyman edition, p. 69). Mill subsequently declares that "all restraint, *qua* restraint, is an evil" (Ch. V, p. 150).

[24] *Leviathan*, Ch. XIV.

[25] *Principles of Ethics* (New York: D. Appleton, 1897), Vol. II, p. 45. Cf. *Social Statics Abridged and Revised* (New York: D. Appleton, 1897), p. 55. Spencer regards this as the basic "formula of justice" and declares that it is an "axiomatic truth."

[26] *Principles of Political Right*, in Kant's *Principles of Politics*, trans. W. Hastie (Edinburgh: Clark, 1891), p. 36. For other formulations of this principle by Kant see pp. 12, 34, 39, 48 of the Hastie volume; also *Philosophy of Law* (trans. W. Hastie [Edinburgh: Clark, 1887], pp. 45-46, "Universal Principle of Right"); *Critique of Pure Reason*, A316 = B373, trans. N. K. Smith (London: The Macmillan Company, 1933), p. 312.

[27] *On Liberty*, Ch. I (Everyman edition, p. 75).

(5) ". . . there is at least one natural right, the equal right of all men to be free . . . any human being capable of choice (1) has the right to forbearance on the part of all others from the use of coercion or restraint against him save to hinder coercion or restraint and (2) is at liberty to do . . . any action which is not one coercing or restraining or designed to injure other persons." (H. L. A. Hart) [28]

(6) "That principle is, that the sole end for which mankind are warranted, individually or collectively, in interfering with the liberty of action of any of their number, is self-protection. That the only purpose for which power can be rightfully exercised over any member of a civilised community, against his will, is to prevent harm to others." (J. S. Mill)[29]

(7) " 'In the republic,' says the Marquis d'Argenson, 'each person is perfectly free in that which does not harm others.' This is the invariable limitation; one cannot put it more exactly." (Rousseau) [30]

(8) "Liberty consists in being able to do all that which does not harm someone else; thus, the existence of the natural rights of each man has no limits except those which assure to the other members of the society the enjoyment of these same rights. These limits can only be determined by law." (Declaration of the Rights of Man and the Citizen, Art. 5)

(9) "What do we really mean when we speak of 'Justice'? . . . an equal distribution of the burden of citizenship, i.e. of those limitations of freedom which are necessary in social life . . ." (K. R. Popper) [31]

(10) "In place of the old bourgeois society, with its classes and class antagonisms, we shall have an association in which the free development of each is the condition for the free development of all." (Marx and Engels) [32]

Each of these statements contains, more or less explicitly, two

---

[28] "Are There Any Natural Rights?" *Philosophical Review*, LXIV (1955), p. 175.
[29] *On Liberty*, Ch. I (Everyman edition, pp. 72-73).
[30] *Social Contract*, IV, viii (Everyman edition, p. 120 n.).
[31] *The Open Society and Its Enemies*, 2nd ed. (London: Routledge, 1952), Vol. I, p. 89.
[32] *The Communist Manifesto*, II (fin.).

components. One is affirmative: all men should be equally free to do as they like. Although the meaning of "freedom" may vary, it includes at least the ability to act without external restraint.[33] This absence of external restraint may be signified either directly negatively, as independence of control by someone else, or positively, as obedience to directions one has given oneself. These two formulations have the same meaning, for one's acts, insofar as they have moral relevance, must be directed or controlled by one or more human beings, and if such controller is not other persons then it must be the agent himself.[34]

The second component of all the formulas is crucial, for it sets forth the principle by which the otherwise unrestrained freedom indicated in the first component is to be justly restrained by governmental or legal controls. There are at least three different kinds of such limiting conditions in the passages quoted above, so that there are at least three different interpretations of the principle of equal freedom as a principle of political justice.

According to the first interpretation, which I shall call the *specific act* interpretation, a man is free to do any act so long as his doing it does not prevent other men from doing the same kind of act. This interpretation is found in Spencer and in the second part of the first sentence quoted from the Declaration of the Rights of Man. Within this general interpretation, various species are possible. One may or may not, for example, add the words "to him," such that A is free to do any act he likes to B so long as his doing it does not prevent B from doing the same kind of act to him. This last seems to be the meaning of Hobbes' statement.

[33] This meaning is found, not only in such obvious cases as Hobbes and J. S. Mill, but also in Kant ("Freedom is independence of the compulsory will of another," *Philosophy of Law*, "Introduction to the Science of Right" [trans. Hastie, p. 56]) and in Rousseau ("Obedience to the law which one has prescribed to oneself is liberty," *Social Contract*, I, viii).

[34] Sir Isaiah Berlin has called attention, in his important *Two Concepts of Liberty* (Oxford University Press, 1958), to some of the ways in which the "positive" interpretation has lent itself to authoritarian perversions. Such perversions, however, are in my opinion not inevitable; early in his monograph (p. 16) Sir Isaiah recognizes that, in their basic formulations, the negative and positive interpretations are logically equivalent. However, see also below, p. 168f.

According to the second interpretation, which I shall call the *general libertarian* interpretation, a man is free to do any act so long as his doing it does not infringe the freedom of others, *i.e.*, so long as his doing it does not prevent others from doing (or being free to do) whatever acts they may want to do. This interpretation is found in Kant and in all save the last clause of Hart's statement; it is also found in the first statement from Mill. The limiting condition may be either the infringement of freedom in general or the infringement of particular freedoms, and each of these either for a society as a whole or for one or more individuals within the society.

The specific act interpretation and the general libertarian interpretation are quite different from one another. The freedom of others to do whatever they may want to do is a more extensive concept than is the ability or freedom to do the same kind of act to others as others do to oneself. For example, both the specific act interpretation and the general libertarian interpretation exclude murder from the sphere of permitted acts. But the specific act interpretation does not rule out physical assault, or cheating: *A* is free to cheat *B* or to assault *B* physically so long as this leaves *B* free (subsequently) to cheat or assault *A* or others.[35] But according to the general libertarian interpretation, *A* is not free to cheat or assault *B* at all, since this would diminish or infringe *B*'s freedom to do other things. Moreover if, with Kant, we generalize the freedom to assault someone into a "universal law" that each person may cheat or assault others whenever he likes, this would obviously cut down on the total freedom within the society, even though each

---

[35] Spencer tried to avoid these consequences of the specific act interpretation; see *Principles of Ethics*, Vol. II, p. 46. But in so doing, he changed it into a different principle, where one of the decisive considerations is "actions which . . . conduce to the maintenance of his life." This change was pointed out by Sidgwick in his incisive critique of Spencer's formula; see *Lectures on the Ethics of T. H. Green, Mr. Herbert Spencer, and J. Martineau* (London: The Macmillan Company, 1902), p. 272. Sidgwick presented detailed criticisms of the principle of equal freedom in his major writings. See *Methods of Ethics*, 5th ed., Book III, Ch. V (London: The Macmillan Company, 1893), pp. 274-79; *Elements of Politics*, 4th ed., Ch. IV (London: The Macmillan Company, 1919), pp. 44ff.; and cf. *Principles of Political Economy*, 3rd ed. (London: The Macmillan Company, 1901), pp. 405-406.

victim of cheating or assault might subsequently be free to reciprocate in kind against his offender or others.[36]

The specific act interpretation seems to provide the most obviously egalitarian answer to the problem of the just limits of
freedom: it is just to deprive someone of his freedom when others
are equally deprived. (The concept of the rule of law obviously is
implicit in this statement.) But this still leaves open the question:
when *is* it just for all (or any) to be equally deprived of their freedom to do some act? That such deprivation must be equal is indeed a necessary condition of just restraints on action, but that it
is not a sufficient condition is shown by the acts permitted by the
specific act interpretation.

Furthermore, the general libertarian interpretation provides support for the civil liberties of speech, press, and assembly involved
in the method of consent, and also for other liberties, such as religion. The specific act interpretation, on the other hand, does not
rule out from the range of just acts the prevention of others from
speaking or otherwise expressing their ideas. Nor, applied to the
relation between government and private individuals, does it rule
out the ability of the rulers to repress freedoms of speech, press,
assembly, religion, so long as, when the rulers become subjects,
they likewise undergo repression in these areas. The general
libertarian interpretation not only rules out such repression, it also
removes from governmental control an immense array of other
human pursuits, including such matters as family arrangements,
sexual conduct, many economic affairs, the cultivation of the arts
and sciences, and so on. It emphasizes the absolute value of freedom:
the only limitation of the individual's freedom is to be the general
freedom of others. To be sure, subtle problems may be raised about
the principle's application to each of these areas: does not a man's
winning of a wife or of a certain job infringe the freedom of others
to have that same wife or job? Such problems can be solved, however, by a suitable universalizing of the relevant terms: the freedom

---

[36] In an appendix to *Principles of Ethics* (Vol. II, pp. 437-39), Spencer discussed the relation between his formulation of the equal freedom principle
and Kant's; but he does not seem to have noted the differences pointed out
above.

of others to win *some* wife or job is not infringed (conditions presumed not to be abnormal). The general libertarian interpretation, with its pluralist consequences for society as consisting in a multiplicity of individuals and groups each pursuing their own values in their own way, simply emphasizes the absolute value of freedom: the only limitation of the individual's freedom is to be the general freedom of others.

Yet this libertarian position is not a sufficient criterion either of political justice in general or of the just limitation of governmental restraints on individual freedom. To see this, consider a third interpretation of the limiting condition in the principle of equal freedom as presented in some of the passages quoted above. According to this interpretation, which I shall call the "negative utilitarian" one, a man is free to do any act so long as his doing it does not harm someone else. This interpretation is found in the second passage quoted from Mill, in the passage from Rousseau, in the very last clause of Hart's statement, and in the first clause quoted from the Declaration of Rights. The *someone else* who must not be harmed may be taken to be either one or more individuals or the whole society. There is, of course, an intimate connection between these two kinds of harm, but the "social" species seems predominant in Rousseau and Popper.

The negative utilitarian interpretation differs from the specific act interpretation by ruling out all acts of physical assault as such, as well as stealing, cheating, and so on, simply because such acts are harmful to their victims, regardless of the ability of the latter to reciprocate in kind. Its difference from the general libertarian interpretation may be less clear, for it might seem that to infringe the freedom of others is to harm them. But is it not sometimes good for a person that he be deprived of the freedom to do certain acts? Obvious examples of such acts are committing suicide, selling oneself into slavery, or driving across a bridge which is about to collapse. In such cases the individual's freedom of action is justly restrained because of the harm it would do him. It may be argued, as Mill does,[37] that the harm in such cases consists precisely in the subsequent loss of freedom to which such acts would lead. There

[37] *On Liberty,* Ch. V (Everyman edition, pp. 151-52, 157-58).

are many other kinds of acts, however, which do not infringe the
liberty of others but which are, or may be, harmful to them, so that
while such acts would be permitted by the general libertarian interpretation they are prohibited by the negative utilitarian interpretation. This can be illustrated by a passage from Justice Holmes'
famous dissent in the Lochner case:

> The liberty of the citizen to do as he likes so long as he does not inter-
> fere with the liberty of others to do the same, which has been a shib-
> boleth for some well-known writers, is interfered with by school laws,
> by the Post Office, by every State or municipal institution which takes
> his money for purposes thought desirable, whether he likes it or not.
> The Fourteenth Amendment does not enact Mr. Herbert Spencer's
> *Social Statics*.[38]

In this passage Holmes is referring primarily to what I have called
the "specific act" version of the principle of equal freedom, and
the consideration he adduces for overriding it is not the negative
one of harmfulness but the more positive-sounding idea of "purposes
thought desirable." This consideration, however, also applies against
the general libertarian position: what Holmes is saying is that
government has the right to interfere with men's freedom to act
even though their acts do not infringe the freedom of others, and
this because of the "desirable purposes" that would be served by
such interference. Moreover, these "purposes" can also be viewed
in negative terms, as the prevention of harm to others or to the
community such as would result from the non-education of children,
the lapse of postal communication, the non-collection of garbage,
and similar causes.

This negative utilitarian interpretation might be assimilated to
that of general libertarianism by arguing that an act or omission
such as a man's refusal to allow his children to be educated harms
others precisely because it infringes their freedom, for it imposes on
them, or on the community, the burden of rectifying the results of
his children's non- or miseducation. This argument raises a general
question about the relation between "freedom" and such values as
literacy or education. Why should "others" be concerned if some,

[38] *Lochner* v. *New York* (1905) 198 U.S. 45.

or even most, members of the community are illiterate? It may be replied that it is because the literate members would have to make up for the deficiencies of the illiterates in respect of the many affairs of the community for which literacy is required; and this too is why wide-spread illiteracy would infringe the freedom of the literate persons. But is not the insistence of the literate ones that the rest become literate and send their children to school, equally an infringement on the freedom of the illiterates? If the principle of justice is that of equal freedom in the general libertarian sense that no one can justly be restrained from any act or failure to act so long as this does not infringe the freedom of others, then why should the freedom of the literate ones be considered above that of the illiterates? This question cannot be answered so long as all freedoms are regarded as being on a par as far as possible governmental restraint or non-restraint is concerned, with the sole criterion for just governmental interference being whether a given freedom infringes the freedom of others. Other values besides freedom must be considered in determining the spheres in which government may justly intervene to restrict freedom.

Another way to give a libertarian interpretation of the justice of considering the freedom of literate persons above that of illiterates might be to point out that the range of effective freedom for illiterates is far smaller since they are unable to utilize the many aids to action provided by literacy. Such an argument, however, contains a meaning of "freedom" different from the one followed so far, for it involves not merely the negative absence of external restraint but the positive ability to act. While, as we saw above, the negative and positive definitions of "freedom" as, respectively, absence of external restraints and self-determination are logically equivalent, this equivalence is sharply reduced in a dynamic or comparative analysis. For to be "more free" in the sense of there being fewer external restraints to one's action is not necessarily the same as being "more free" in the sense of determining or being able to determine oneself more fully. The latter involves the acquisition by the individual, through education or other means, of more abilities than he had before. It hence implies a change within him and not merely the removal of obstacles external to him. Consequently, if the relation of government to individual freedom is at issue, then whereas on the negative interpretation of "freedom" the government would be obliged to refrain from imposing requirements like literacy on the individual, on the positive interpretation the government's obligation would be to impose such requirements: and the more such requirements were imposed, the freer the individual might be.

The obvious argument for the consideration of the freedom of literate persons above the freedom of illiterates to refrain from sending their children to school is the harm to the community that illiteracy involves. This, of course, is the argument advanced even by convinced libertarians.[39] Consequently, the purely formal answer to the problem of the just limits of governmental restraints provided by the first two interpretations of the principle of equal freedom is not sufficient. A concept like "harm" involves substantive value-considerations over and above the negative sense of freedom. This amounts to saying not only that freedom is not the only value, but also that the political rights whose equal distribution constitutes justice include considerations which are closely related to, if they are not identical with, welfare or beneficence.

The Principle of the Common Good

The discussion in the preceding section reached a conclusion apparently quite antithetical to the question with which it began. Its question was that of the just limits of political power, but the answer that finally emerged seemed to involve an expansion rather than a limitation of power. To be sure, it might be expressed as a limitation: governmental interference with individual freedom should be limited to those cases where an individual's action or inaction is harmful to others or to the community. But even if we further specify this so as to exclude many kinds of acts harmful only to individuals, this still leaves a very large and indeterminate area for governmental regulation. For, depending on how "harm" is defined, almost any degree of governmental control can be

[39] Cf. F. A. Hayek, *The Constitution of Liberty* (Chicago, Ill.: University of Chicago Press, 1960), pp. 376-77.

justified by this formula. In fact, all governments, even the most repressive ones, have justified their activities on the ground either of preventing harm or of promoting the good of the community.[40]

There is, of course, a difference between preventing harm or disutility and increasing good or utility. Formally, it may be said that all cases of preventing harm are cases of doing good, although not conversely. But it is very difficult to draw the line between these in the sociopolitical sphere. The educational system, old-age pensions, weather forecasting, care of orphans, the building of new roads for more and faster automobiles—do these prevent harm or promote the common good? In part, the answer depends on the expectations, values, and resources of the community. As Justice Cardozo put it, "Nor is the concept of the general welfare static. Needs that were narrow or parochial a century ago may be interwoven in our day with the well-being of the nation. What is critical or urgent changes with the times." [41]

The traditional models of governmental activity have varied from a minimal, passive government restricted to reacting against crimes ("harms") already committed, to a maximal, active government that controls as much as possible of the lives of its members in the name of the common good, or the public interest, or the general welfare.[42] This range is reflected in the ambiguity of the word

---

[40] "I think, however, that we may go a step further, and claim general—if not universal—assent for the principle that the true criterion by which right legislation is to be distinguished from wrong is conduciveness to the general 'good' or 'welfare' " (H. Sidgwick, *Elements of Politics,* 4th ed. [London: The Macmillan Company, 1919], p. 38).

[41] *Helvering* v. *Davis* (1937) 301 U.S. 619.

[42] These three expressions obviously belong to a common family. There are subtle differences between them; for example, "public" has a more political connotation than "common" or "general"; and "welfare" nowadays often has the specific meaning of governmental assistance to the unfortunate. In what follows, however, I shall for the most part use these expressions interchangeably. In recent years "the public interest" has come to be used much more frequently than "the common good," at least in the United States. The reasons for this include perhaps the fact that "interest" can have a triple use: as a noun in the plural, "interests" is a word that can be used to signify both diverse pressure-groups and their specific goals, while "the public interest," although taking cognizance of such considerations, can be used to refer to purposes which should override these because they may affect everybody. This triple use of "interest" is already found in Federalist No. 10. For surveys of recent discussions of "the public interest," see W. A. R. Leys and C. M.

"promotes" in such a familiar expression as that "a just government promotes (or acts for) the common good." For this can mean
either (a) "everything that is done by the government must be for
the common good," or (b) "everything that is for the common good
must be done by the government." The problem of the common
good as a principle of political justice is in part that of avoiding
the totalitarian implications of (b) without falling into a too restrictive interpretation of (a). More generally, it is the problem of indi-
cating the criteria for regarding acts as affecting the community for
"good" and for "harm," and of specifying what should be the relation of government to such acts. The importance of the principle
of the common good as a distinct principle of political justice is
that it focuses attention on the question of what political power
should be for, what it should do, as against what it should not do.
This requires a positive conception of human well-being and of the
contribution which government can make to it.

Political justice is equality of political rights, and each principle
of political justice presents a criterion for the achievement of such
equality. But whereas in the principle of consent the individual is
viewed as a participant in the source of political power leading to
the decision-making process, and in the principle of equal freedom
the individual is viewed in respect of his non-restraint by the results
of the process, in the principle of the common good the individual
is viewed as a participant in these results, in the affirmative ends of
political power. All three principles are concerned with the rights
of citizenship, but in consent it is the "active" rights that are
involved, in equal freedom it is the negative "passive" rights, and
in the common good it is the positive "passive" rights.

There are at least two objections to the view that the common
good can be a principle of political justice. The first argues that
justice is only one virtue among others; but if it is equated with
the common good then the boundary between it and moral goodness or rightness disappears and justice becomes synonymous with

---

Perry, *Philosophy and the Public Interest* (Chicago, Ill.: Committee to Advance
Original Work in Philosophy, 1959), and G. Schubert, *The Public Interest*
(Glencoe, Ill.: Free Press, 1960). For a discussion of some of the traditional problems about the common good, see B. de Jouvenel, *Sovereignty: An Inquiry into
the Political Good* (Cambridge: Cambridge University Press, 1957), Ch. 7.

the whole of morality. To this objection there are at least three replies. First, the common good is here being considered not as a definition of political justice but as a criterion of it or as a means of attaining it. Second, there is a difference between the common good, the public interest or utility, and the goods, interests, or utilities which individuals have in their private capacities. Third, although political justice in its relation to the common good or the public interest is a part of morality in the broad sense of the word, it is concerned primarily with external actions and not with the inner intentions and motivations that are basic to moral goodness and also, at least in part, to moral rightness.

A second objection to the common good as a principle of political justice is that this is to make a further confusion between distributive principles and aggregative principles. Justice is a distributive principle in that it concerns the distribution of benefits or burdens to individuals or groups on some such basis as desert or need. But the common good is an aggregative principle in that its concern is not with what befits or is owed to individuals or groups as such, but rather with what is beneficial to the whole community.[43] But, although there is a difference between a distributive and an aggregative principle, the use of the word "justice," especially in political contexts, is not so invariant that it can be immediately classified under the distributive principle. A law or a governmental act is sometimes held to be just if it is for the general welfare, even if it adversely affects the needs or interests of various particular groups within the community. But this point can also be put in distributive terms: political power is just if it distributes burdens and rewards in a way that is conducive to the common good, or if its rules or laws are conducive to the common good.[44]

[43] Cf. B. M. Barry, "Justice and the Common Good," *Analysis*, XXI (1961), pp. 86-90.
[44] The view that the common good or the public interest is a principle of political justice has strong historical support. It is at least as old as Aristotle, who wrote that "governments which aim at the common interest are in accord with absolute justice," and again that "the political good is justice, that is, the common interest" (*Politics* III, 6, 1279a18; III, 12, 1282b17). A similar alliance of justice with public utility is found in Hume and is, of course, basic to the utilitarians. For other references to political justice as consisting in the common good, see *The Federalist*, Nos. 10 and 34 (New York: Modern Library), pp. 59, 208.

For justice consists in giving men that to which they have a right, and on the egalitarian criterion of such right men have a right to a government which acts for the common good and not for its own private advantage or for that of some group in the community as against others. This right belongs to each man individually and to the whole community collectively. Locke defined political power as "a right of making laws . . . only for the public good," [45] and this meant that the public and the community had a correlative right that the holders of political power act for the public good.

What, then, is "the common good"? Is the common good anything more than the private interests of individuals or groups? Is there any way of finding out what are the goods or interests of persons other than by seeing what they actually desire or pursue? If the common good is what these interests have in common, then is it not very slight, since individual or group interests are often in conflict? If any action or policy which promotes the common good is just, then may not justice entail violating the rights of individuals, since the common good may sometimes be promoted by such violation?

Such questions hinge initially on the meanings of "common" and "good." Each of these words has a range of meanings that covers two extreme alternatives and various possible intermediate meanings. In the case of "common," the extremes are individualist (or "nominalist") and corporatist (or organic or "Platonic realist"). According to the individualist extreme, a community consists simply in its individual members, so that the common good can be only some sort of sum or aggregate of the goods of individuals. According to the corporatist extreme, a community has a reality independent of its members, so that the common good is the good of this corporate being. In the case of "good," the extremes are subjective and objective. According to the subjective extreme, something is good if it is an object of desire or approval by some person or group. According to the objective extreme, something is good if it is valuable or desirable, independently of whether it is in fact valued or desired. A subjective interpretation of "good" can be combined with a corporatist interpretation of "common," as

[45] *Second Treatise of Civil Government,* sec. 3.

when the common good is held to be what is desired by the nation, conceived as an entity distinct from its component individual members. And an objective interpretation of "good" can be combined with an individualist interpretation of "common," as when the common good is held to be what is objectively desirable for the individuals who make up the community.

No one combination of these meanings is uniquely right or wrong; different ones are applicable in different contexts. And from this there follows a further point: that, parallel to these different meanings, there are different appropriate methods of promoting the common good, ranging from rigorous governmental control to a minimum of control.

Consider first an approach which, unlike the one just proposed, defines the common good in terms of a single set of factors related more or less closely to the method of consent. By such a definition the question of what methods should be used by government to promote the common good is automatically answered. This approach has two distinctive features. First, its procedural emphasis: it insists that the common good can be given only a procedural definition, that the concept can have no substantive content. Second, its "groupist" emphasis: it views the common good in terms of the opposed interests of competing pressure groups, so that there is no "common" good in the sense of one that pertains to the whole community. It can be seen that these features are specifications, respectively, of the subjective and individualist interpretations of the common good. On this view, then, the common good is defined as whatever emerges from the democratic decision-making process of conflicting pressures and compromises among competing groups.[46] And it is by this process that the role to be taken by government in promoting the common good is to be ascertained.

This approach derives much of its strength from the fact that it views political controversy over immediate issues as the sole context for defining the common good. Its motivation is in large part a

---

[46] An approach of this kind is defended in various ways by Schubert and by the "realists" whom he sympathetically analyzes, *op. cit.*, Chs. IV and V. See also H. R. Smith, *Democracy and the Public Interest* (Athens, Ga.: University of Georgia Press, 1960).

methodological or epistemological one, for group processes or operations are directly amenable to empirical inquiry. The various pressures that different groups exert in the decision-making process can be observed and compared and the common good therefore given an empirical and even quantitative content, as against the subjective, moralistic, and unverifiable characteristics it would otherwise have. Nevertheless, this approach has serious limitations, for to define the common good in terms of the process or results of democratic decision-making overlooks the significant difference in meaning between these two concepts. For it is not self-contradictory to say that the decision reached by the democratic process turned out not to be for the common good. And it is not tautological to say that what the democratic process was trying to achieve, or at least the standard by which it is to be evaluated, is the common good.

While this argument is somewhat similar to Moore's "open question" test,[47] it is not designed to establish that all attempts to define the common good must commit a fallacy. It involves rather a more specific point about the relation between purposive-process terms and substantive-result terms. If a process may be viewed as aiming at a certain substantive result, such that the process is to be evaluated by its success in achieving that result, then the envisaged result cannot be defined in terms of the process for the process would by definition already contain the result.

It may be replied that the process was not aiming at any substantive result. But then was it aiming only at itself? Or at nothing? The situation here is similar to that found in Justice Holmes' famous definition of law as "the prophecies of what the courts will do in fact." [48] For on this definition it makes no sense to say that what the courts do or ought to do is to consult the law in order to reach their decision. If the judicial process may or should be based on the law, as the political process may or should *aim at* the common good, then it makes no sense to say that what "the law" or "the common good" means is either the process itself or whatever emerges from the process.

[47] See G. E. Moore, *Principia Ethica* (Cambridge: Cambridge University Press, 1903), Ch. I.
[48] *Collected Legal Papers* (Boston, Mass.: Little, Brown, 1920), p. 173.

The point of the groupist emphasis of this approach is in part that, so far as sociopolitical phenomena are concerned, "the public" or "the community" is but a fiction; all that really exists is conflicting pressure groups. On this view the democratic process becomes one of rhetorical manipulation: alleged considerations of truth, goodness, or beauty are but so many group weapons that must make their way in the political battleground or market-place. Morally, its point is that if the political sphere is not viewed in this way, if claims to social truth or value are credited as being objectively determinable outside the democratic process, then democratic egalitarianism is endangered and sinister kinds of authoritarianism may be encouraged. Intellectually, its point is that there is no way to determine truth in the sphere of political issues other than by such opposition of group pressures.

These points, however, are not cogent if an adequate view is taken of the democratic community and the processes, including moral and cognitive ones which it helps to make possible. Many interests are obviously common to a whole society—not only procedural ones like the rule of law, but substantive ones like order, security, and basic economic needs. Even if diversified within various segments of the society, they are still sufficiently homogeneous to be called common. The possibility of adequate, impartial knowledge on public issues involves no danger of authoritarianism if a distinction is drawn between intellectual and political values and if the democratic process is maintained as the basis of political decision-making: democratic values can be enhanced through the free rein they give to attempts to shed cognitive light on social issues. One of the main difficulties of the groupist approach is that it uses the concept of pressure to deal with all forces operative in society, intellectual as well as political. The concept is itself very confused. As many current social scientists use the term, "pressure" becomes synonymous with almost any kind of causation. So long as a component of behavior can exert any kind of influence on someone else, it is a kind of pressure. As a consequence, in theories which focus on this concept, as in Gresham's law, the least worthy forms of pressure tend to drive out the best: all are reduced to the lowest common denominator. No distinctions are drawn as to the rational

contents or methods of different kinds of pressure. Threats of political retaliation, suggestions for compromise, rhetorical flourishes,
statements of fact or of causal relations all become just so many
different forms of pressure. The idea of truth about social questions
is transformed into the outcome of conflicting pressures, and the
possibility of securing disinterested knowledge which may serve to
guide public policy on matters affecting the common good is ignored.

These considerations emphasize that it is important not to confuse four distinct questions about the common good. What does
"the common good" mean? Is it possible to know what is for the
common good? How are political decisions concerning the common
good arrived at? How should these decisions be arrived at—or, at
least, how can they be improved? The approach just considered
really gives only a partial answer to the third question. But because
its upholders also thought that it was answering the other questions
as well, they could see no point in any substantive definition of
the common good.

Such a substantive interpretation may approach the common
good from two different directions: the private wants of individuals
and the needs of society. The former begins from the subjective
and individualist poles of the meaning of "common good," while
the latter begins from the objective and corporatist poles. Although
the emphases of these approaches are different, some of the components which they include in the common good coincide.

If the common good is approached from the standpoint of the
contents of goods directly desired by individuals, there can be distinguished six different ways in which there can be said to be
"common goods." These turn on several variables as to how things
can be called "common" and "good": not only the pairs of alternatives indicated above but also such others as means-end, immediate-
remote, prudential-moral.

One kind of common good consists of numerically diverse but
qualitatively identical or similar objects such that each individual
possesses and enjoys a numerically different one of these objects.
The most obvious examples of such objects are material things:
articles of clothing, foodstuffs, reading matter. But personal or

individual freedoms may also be put in this class, insofar as they are freedoms which each individual has or may have to act (or refrain from acting as he sees fit). It was for this reason that Locke classed liberty as well as life and estate under "property." Each of these objects is a "common good," not in the sense that each person has the numerically same shoes or toothbrush or freedom, but in the sense that each has and values his own. Here "common" is a distributive or individualist word; it refers to what is separately had by each person.

Another kind of common good consists of objects which individuals can have or use collectively rather than distributively, such as a public park. The park is a "common" good, not in the sense that each person has his own park or some small part of it, but in the sense that each has the use of the whole park. Here, "common" is a collective word so far as possession of the park is concerned, but it may still be a distributive word so far as use of the park is concerned; each person may enjoy it separately.

A third kind of common good consists in the values of interpersonal communication itself. Here the common object of value is itself human; it consists in shared appreciation of anything from the simplest pleasures to the loftiest ideals, but the sharing is at least as important as what is shared. It may be found in a formal organization like a social club or a college or it may be found in a much more informal relationship, ranging from long-standing friendships to casual meetings. Human community is an intrinsic requirement of such common goods, whereas in the first two kinds of common good it is required primarily as a means to what is valued rather than as the object of value itself.

A fourth kind of common good consists in the whole environmental context which provides the indispensable means to common goods of the first three kinds. This context is of two sorts: nonhuman (physical and biological) and human (the economic, legal, and political framework of the community). Whereas each of the first three kinds of common good was assimilable with little or no difficulty to the subjective meaning of "good" (by being directly valued or enjoyed either as end or as means), this kind of common good may not be directly valued or enjoyed at all; in fact, the individuals in question may not even be conscious of it. Yet as the necessary means to the other goods, its goodness is more objective than subjective. And it is corporate rather than individualist. The economic, legal, and political framework of the community involves certain ways of relating individuals to one another, and this relation is not simply reducible to the individuals related.

The goodness of each of the first four kinds of common good consisted either in its being directly had and valued by individuals or in its being a necessary means to such direct objects of value. The goodness of the fifth kind of common good is more an ideal: what men would value as an end if they were more educated or otherwise more enlightened. It was partly in this sense that Mill declared that his "ultimate appeal" would be to "utility in the largest sense, grounded on the permanent interests of man as a progressive being." [49] It was in this sense, too, that the chairman of the Federal Communications Commission, criticizing the television networks for giving the public a steady diet of trash, asserted that the public interest is not the same as "what interests the public." [50]

The sixth kind of common good is also ideal, but the ideal in question is moral. Whereas the first five kinds of common goods were had or to be had solely by the individuals or groups to whom they were common, this sixth kind requires consideration of the good of others, and for their sakes. An example of such a moral common good is the economic aid which an affluent society gives to less fortunate societies. Such a policy may or may not coincide with the society's prudential interest in winning friends and removing threatening tensions.

All six kinds of common goods are substantive in that they have a definitive content which can be specified. To say that some of these are desired or otherwise valued is to introduce a subjective element; but the desires in question are either so universal or else so defensible on moral, intellectual, or other grounds that no spe-

---

[49] On Liberty, Ch. I. (Everyman edition, p. 74).

[50] "What do we mean by 'the public interest'? Some say the public interest is what interests the public. I disagree" (N. N. Minow, Speech before the National Association of Broadcasters, reprinted in Chicago Sun-Times, May 21, 1961, Sec. 2, p. 1).

cial reference to a desiderative factor seems necessary. On the other hand, these six kinds are not equally relevant to political problems. The order in which the six kinds of common goods were listed was determined by an individualist-subjective approach which began from the private enjoyments of individuals and gradually branched out to their necessary social conditions; it arrived only at the last at goods completely devoid of egocentric reference.

Viewed from a social point of view, common goods may be distinguished into three groups, consisting in the necessary conditions (1) for the preservation of any society, (2) for the preservation of the distinctive sociopolitical values of a specific kind of society, and (3) for extending or advancing these values. The content of each of these conditions varies with circumstances. The necessary conditions for the preservation of any society include internal and external order and security and provision for economic needs, including food, clothing, shelter. The necessary conditions for the preservation of the distinctive sociopolitical values of a specific society can be illustrated by the difference between the conditions of survival of the United States and of the Soviet Union, as such. The abolition of political and intellectual freedom in the United States, for example, would entail "its" destruction, and the introduction of such freedom in the Soviet Union would have the same effect there, because in each case there is a basic change in the respective constitutional and moral structures. As this example suggests, the distinctive sociopolitical values of a society comprise neither its doctrines of social morality alone nor its actual institutions alone, but rather that combination of the two whereby each dynamically interacts with the other. In a liberal democracy, doctrines of social morality can have a powerful effect on institutions, as was seen, for example, in the Supreme Court school desegregation decision. The necessary conditions for extending these values are along the same lines.

Although these three kinds of necessary conditions may overlap to some extent, they form in general a hierarchy somewhat similar to the hierarchies of needs elaborated not only by anthropologists and sociologists but also by psychologists. That fulfillment of the first kind of necessary condition is a prerequisite to the second has been graphically illustrated throughout history: in recent times by the demoralization of the Weimar regime in Germany during the economic disasters of the period following the First World War, and the threatened collapse of democratic institutions in the United States during the Great Depression. This hierarchic relation has sometimes been dangerously ignored in United States foreign policy, when it has demanded that impoverished nations adopt democratic institutions as the basis for receiving aid and friendship. This hierarchic order of priorities also extends both to their relative degree of non-controversialness or objectivity and to the role of government in regard to them. National survival and internal order are imperative common goods for which all possible means must be taken by government, although these will always be weighed in the light of the other two kinds of conditions.

In a liberal democracy, all three of these kinds of necessary conditions are open to debate. But a distinction must be drawn between means and ends. The ends in question are not themselves open to dispute; it is the relative merits of various proposed measures to achieve these ends that are debated. As the ends are more clearly understood, knowledge of how to attain them becomes increasingly available, and this knowledge can give to the ends a substantive content.

Among these ends, the preservation of democratic procedures is of central importance. But a distinction must again be drawn, this time between procedures themselves and what is left to be settled by procedures. Whether political decisions should be reached by the democratic procedure cannot itself be left to that procedure. The procedure is on a higher level, so to speak, than the decisions which are left open to be decided by it. Hence the preservation of democratic procedure is one of the main components in the democratic common good.

If democratic methods served no ends beyond themselves they would still be, as methods, preferable to all others. But to emphasize them regardless of context is to ignore the fact that there are unfortunate circumstances, still frequent in many parts of the world, where certain minimal ends are so far from being achieved and democratic methods so inapplicable that it is futile to urge them. The fact that such economic values as improved standards of living and such sociological values as increase of mutual trust can be specified as ends for the method to aim at shows that the common good has a substantive content which is, as such, independent of the policies or procedures which may be used to attain them. This is the case even though the democratic method may be the safest as well as the most effective way of achieving these values.

These two different substantive approaches to the common good —one beginning from the private wants of individuals, the other beginning from the needs of society—can be synthesized in a way which, while still substantive, emphasizes better than either of them taken alone the specific values of the liberal democratic tradition. Such a synthesis focuses on the question: Of what kinds of persons ought the democratic community to be composed? This question brings out the double point that the common good as viewed in the liberal democratic context consists ultimately in certain value-attributes of individuals, and that these attributes are not individualistic in the sense of egocentric but are oriented within the framework of a community. The function of a just government is to foster these attributes, but in ways that take account of, and hence are limited by, the values themselves.

Among the many components that have traditionally figured in the varying answers to this question, some are specifically political, involving interest and participation in public affairs and the like. But such components are in important respects only means to more ultimate moral considerations; for, after all, there may be kinds of political interest and participation which are antithetical to democratic values and to a democratic conception of the common good. What, then, are these more ultimate moral considerations? They are focused on the freedom and intelligence of individuals who can think for themselves and who have the knowledge and ability to follow out their own conceptions of the good life, in ways that are also socially useful and respect the equal rights of others. Four aspects of this conception must be emphasized. First, a democratic government has an active commitment to an intelligent, well-informed citizenry. Second, freedom as envisaged here is coupled with "ability"; it involves not only absence of restraint but possession of positive means to act toward one's goals; and it includes freedom of thought in both respects. Third, the respect for the equal rights of others is an indispensable moral component. Fourth, social utility, while it should be very broadly conceived, indicates the intermeshing of individual interests and contributions to society which makes compatible with one another private and common goods. When properly developed, it includes governmental concern for moral, intellectual, and even aesthetic common goods.

When the common good is viewed as comprising these moral values, it provides a synthesis not only of the individualist and corporatist approaches but also, in large part, of the first two principles of political justice. A government which is just in the sense of promoting such a common good maintains the principles of consent and equal freedom as part of its constitutional structure, and actively seeks to provide for all its members equality of opportunity to achieve all four of the kinds of value listed above. Such equality is itself, therefore, a basic component of the common good. When it is said that some policy is "for" the common good or "promotes" the common good, this sometimes means that it benefits the community as a whole, such as the building of new highways. But at other times the expression has a distributive meaning: that the policy in question will make more "common," in the sense of more equally distributed, certain important goods. Welfare legislation seeks to do this by a variety of methods ranging from distribution of surplus food to the needy to increasing opportunities for higher education for those unable to afford it. Civil rights policies seek to do this by removing some of the obstacles to the enjoyment of political and other freedoms. There may, of course, be variations as to the extent to which some of these goods should be equalized. But in all these cases it is clear that the common good is an egalitarian concept, particularly in that aspect of it which consists in utilizing the resources of the society to provide equality of opportunity for achieving the values which living within the society makes possible.

This egalitarian way of promoting the common good is sometimes held to be justified only as a means to the other, collective way: civil rights legislation, for example, is defended on the ground that it will improve the national reputation or economy. Yet the two kinds of justification are distinct in meaning; and in a liberal democracy where basic equalities are part of the constitutional and moral framework, the egalitarian sense of promoting the common good is sufficient justification of itself.

The values that make up the political common good in a liberal democracy function not only as the ends but also as the limits of democratic political power, in that interference with individual freedom must ultimately be justified by the contribution it makes to these values. A just government both aims at these values and, so far as possible, exhibits them in its own operations. This conception thus combines the individualist and the corporatist conceptions of the common good. While most modern schools of political thought have had a similar optimism about the compatibility of individual and social goods, democratic principles preclude the swallowing up of individual goals in a larger corporate whole. The democratic ideal is one of compatibility between individual happiness and social justice, but with due recognition of the tensions between these goals and of the legitimate disputes about specific means of achieving them. To emphasize only the disputes, however, is to overlook the large substantive content that has already been vindicated for the common good. The disputes occur on the outlying districts, and with regard to these the problematic and procedural emphases are more plausible. Yet even here the past clarifications of ideals serve as indispensable guiding lines.

About the Editor
and Authors

RICHARD B. BRANDT, the editor, is Professor of Philosophy at Swarthmore College, and the author of *Ethical Theory* (1959) and *Hopi Ethics: A Theoretical Analysis* (1954).

WILLIAM K. FRANKENA, Professor of Philosophy at the University of Michigan, is the author of articles on theoretical problems of moral philosophy as well as on several historic figures.

GREGORY VLASTOS, a member of the Institute for Advanced Study at Princeton in 1954-55, is Stuart Professor of Philosophy at Princeton University, and the author of articles on Greek philosophy, social philosophy, and the philosophy of religion.

KENNETH E. BOULDING is Professor of Economics at the University of Michigan. A sometime fellow of the Center for Advanced Study of Behavioral Science at Stanford University, he is the author of *Economic Analysis* (1941), *Economics of Peace* (1945), *A Reconstruction of Economics* (1950), *The Organization Revolution* (1953), *The Image* (1956), *The Skills of the Economist* (1957), *Principles of Economic Policies* (1958).

PAUL A. FREUND, University Professor at Harvard University, has been Pitt Professor of American History and Institutions at Cambridge University. He is author of *On Understanding the Supreme Court* (1949), and is editor-in-chief of *A History of the Supreme Court*.

ALAN GEWIRTH, a Rockefeller Fellow in 1946-47, is Professor of Philosophy at the University of Chicago. He is author of *Marsilius of Padua and Medieval Political Philosophy*.

* Also available in limited clothbound edition.

The American Assembly Series*

S-AA-1   THE FEDERAL GOVERNMENT AND HIGHER EDUCATION, edited by Douglas M. Knight

S-AA-2   THE SECRETARY OF STATE, edited by Don K. Price

S-AA-3   GOALS FOR AMERICANS: THE REPORT OF THE PRESIDENT'S COMMISSION ON NATIONAL GOALS

S-AA-4   ARMS CONTROL: ISSUES FOR THE PUBLIC, edited by Louis Henkin

S-AA-5   OUTER SPACE, edited by Lincoln P. Bloomfield

S-AA-6   THE UNITED STATES AND THE FAR EAST (Second Edition), edited by Willard L. Thorp

S-AA-7   AUTOMATION AND TECHNOLOGICAL CHANGE, edited by John T. Dunlop

Classics in History Series*

S-CH-1   FRONTIER AND SECTION: SELECTED ESSAYS OF FREDERICK JACKSON TURNER, *Introduction and Notes by Ray Allen Billington*

S-CH-2   DRIFT AND MASTERY: AN ATTEMPT TO DIAGNOSE THE CURRENT UNREST, Walter Lippmann, *Introduction and Notes by William E. Leuchtenburg*

S-CH-3   THE NEW NATIONALISM, Theodore Roosevelt, *Introduction and Notes by William E. Leuchtenburg*

S-CH-4   THE NEW FREEDOM: A CALL FOR THE EMANCIPATION OF THE GENEROUS ENERGIES OF A PEOPLE, Woodrow Wilson, *Introduction and Notes by William E. Leuchtenburg*

S-CH-5   EMPIRE AND NATION: JOHN DICKINSON'S "LETTERS FROM A FARMER IN PENNSYLVANIA" AND RICHARD HENRY LEE'S "LETTERS FROM THE FEDERAL FARMER," *Introduction by Forrest McDonald*

S-CH-6   THE SUPREME COURT AND THE CONSTITUTION, Charles A. Beard, *Introduction by Alan F. Westin*

Science and Technology Series*

S-ST-1   THE ATOM AND ITS NUCLEUS, George Gamow

S-ST-2   ROCKET DEVELOPMENT, Robert H. Goddard

S-ST-3   STARS AND GALAXIES: BIRTH, AGEING, AND DEATH IN THE UNIVERSE, Thornton Page

* Also available in limited clothbound edition.

Twentieth Century Views Series*

* Also available in limited clothbound edition.